THE PRACTICAL PILOT

A COMMON SENSE GUIDE TO SAFER FLYING

The Practical Pilot is one of six books by Owen Zupp. His first book, 'Down to Earth', was published in 2006 by Grub Street (UK), while his latest, 'Without Precedent' has been even more widely acclaimed. An award-winning aviation writer, his work has been featured in magazines across the globe including Fly Past (UK), Airliner World (UK), Aviation History (US), Plane & Pilot (US), Global Aviator (South Africa) and Australian Aviation. Owen has won Australasian Aviation Press Club awards and is a commercial pilot with 30 years experience.

www.owenzupp.com

THE PRACTICAL PILOT

OWEN ZUPP

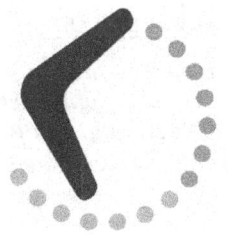

Copyright (c) Owen Zupp 2018

First published in 2018.

Registered Office P.O. Box 747, Bowral NSW 2576. Australia.

Author: Zupp, Owen 1964-

Title: The Practical Pilot. A Pilot's Common Sense Guide to Safer Flying. By Owen Zupp

ISBN: 9 780994 603814

Subjects: Aeroplanes. Piloting. -Biography. Air pilots, -Australia

All rights reserved. No part of this document may be reproduced, stored in a retrieval system, or transmitted in any form or by any means electronic, mechanical, photocopying, recording or otherwise without the permission of the copyright owner.

Cover Image: Cessna 152 in Flight by Steven Pam.

Also by Owen Zupp.

'Without Precedent' - Commando, Fighter Pilot and the true story of Australia's first Purple Heart. (Hardcover, Paperback and eBook)

'50 Tales of Flight' From Biplanes to Boeings. (Paperback and eBook)

'50 More Tales of Flight' (Paperback and eBook)

'Solo Flight' One Pilot's Aviation Adventure around Australia (Paperback and eBook)

'Down to Earth' A Fighter Pilot's Experiences of surviving Dunkirk, the Battle of Britain, Dieppe and D-Day. (Grub Street Publishing. 2007)

Author's Website. www.owenzupp.com

Disclaimer: The content of this text is for the purposes of entertainment and general information only. All aspects of flight operations should be conducted in accordance with the approved operating manuals, company procedures, the relevant regulatory authority and their associated Acts and Regulations.

Contents.

1. CHOOSING A FLYING SCHOOL 1
2. BE PREPARED 7
3. TAKING FLIGHT 14
4. TROUBLES ON TAKE-OFF 24
5. A MATTER OF COURSE 32
6. IN-FLIGHT DIVERSIONS 39
7. FLYING THE APPROACH TO LAND 47
8. LANDING YOUR AIRCRAFT 56
9. THE TRUE MEANING OF PILOT-IN-COMMAND 65
10. THE PILOT'S COMFORT ZONE 72
11. A FORCED LANDING. LESSONS LEARNED 80
12. THE GO-AROUND 90
13. DECISIONS, DECISIONS 98
14. FUEL FOR THOUGHT. PRE-FLIGHT 104
15. FUEL FOR THOUGHT. IN-FLIGHT 112
16. MANAGING IN-FLIGHT EMERGENCIES 121
17. FLYING WITH FRIENDS 130
18. THE VALUE OF CURRENCY 136
19. THE DANGER OF DISTRACTIONS 143
20. TRANSITIONING TO A NEW AIRCRAFT TYPE. 151
21. WELL CHOSEN WORDS. 159
22. PASSING FLIGHT TESTS AND CHECK RIDES 167

About the Author

Owen Zupp is an award-winning writer, published author and commercial pilot with over 20,000 hours of flight time. He has flown all manner of machines from antique biplanes to Boeings and Airbuses and shared the journey with readers around the world in a variety of publications.

The son of a decorated fighter pilot, Owen was born into aviation. His flying career has taken him from outback Australia to the rugged mountain ranges of New Guinea, the idyllic islands of Micronesia and across the oceans of the world. He has served as an airline Captain, Chief Flying Instructor, Chief Pilot and an Approved Test Officer, holding the authority to issue and renew pilot licences and ratings.

Whether witnessing rocket launches from 40,000 feet or circumnavigating a continent for charity in a tiny two-seat training aircraft, Owen has cherished every minute aloft. Flight is not merely his profession; it is his passion.

Foreword

One of the great joys and frustrations is that a pilot will never perfect the art of flight.

Those days when we get close are memorable and those days that we fall short may seem all too frequent. What must be remembered is that the one constant is the challenge. This challenge motivates pilots to continue to work at their craft whether they are on the verge of their first solo flight or at the end of a lengthy career.

We are human, and we will all make mistakes. It is critical that we learn from our mistakes and the oversights of others on our aviation journey. Nobody 'knows it all' and to think otherwise demonstrates a level of complacency that borders on recklessness. Experience is not simply hours in a log book. It is the ability to recognise the need to learn regardless of the years aloft and in turn, to share those lessons.

This book does not override the rules and regulations or the manufacturers' manuals. Rather it seeks to share the lessons from beyond the classroom. Gathered in cockpits and dusty hangars alike, theses chapters are the voices of pilots far and wide. I am indebted to each and every pilot that I have encountered over the last 50 years for they have each made their own special mark. They have each contributed towards writing 'The Practical Pilot'.

Owen Zupp

CHAPTER ONE

Choosing a Flying School

Choosing a flying school is a major first step on your journey in learning to fly. The quality of your flight training is vital and as a customer, you deserve to have certain expectations met. Beyond value-for-money, consistency is also vital. Chopping and changing between aircraft, flight instructors and constant cancellations can impede progress and ultimately cost dollars. Breaking into the aviation industry is never easy, so it's important to make a sound start.

Now I won't pretend for a moment that there's a magical list to suit all scenarios, but what I can offer are some fundamental requirements that your new flying school should provide you with. Prospective aviation students can often feel like overwhelmed novices when they walk into a new flying school and are immediately surrounded by aviators in uniforms and epaulettes speaking a strange dialect known as 'pilot speak'. What is critical at this stage is that you remember that you are a customer and they are attempting to sell you a service, so listen carefully to the real words between the sales pitch and be careful with your cash. Take the time to chat with current students of the school as well.

Also, do your homework first. Research the aviation regulatory body in your part of the world to see what the minimum requirements are to achieve a licence and then bear in mind that these are absolutely MINIMUM LEGAL REQUIREMENTS. You will require more hours of flight training than this and it will equate to a higher cost. Additionally, endeavour to define what level of licence you're seeking. Do you just simply want to go solo to say that you've flown an aeroplane or do you aspire to the flight deck of a Boeing 747? Watch out; you might only want to go solo but find yourself hooked! As such, does the flying school provide comprehensive training all the way through to the commercial pilot's licence and ratings? The internet is a great tool for researching various schools and finding those in your area. Armed with a little prior knowledge about their school and your goals, you're now ready to pay a visit to the local airport and seek out a flying school.

Equipment.

What aircraft does the flying school have? Is there a substantial fleet built upon a few types, or is there a 'Noah's Ark' fleet with seemingly two of every type known to man? What you need is a small range of different types, but enough of the type that you will be training in that it won't be double-booked and leave you stranded or without an aircraft when maintenance falls due. There need to be enough of the aircraft to meet the demands of the school.

Consider the condition of the aircraft. If they are tired and worn out, then that doesn't suggest much re-investment into the fleet by management. It may be a possible indication of cash-flow issues and a signal that corners might be getting cut elsewhere. Either way, a scrappy looking aeroplane does not reflect the mind-set of a proficient, meticulous pilot, nor does it provide the sort of craft in which you'd like to take a family member aloft.

Remember, equipment is not limited to aeroplanes. What are the offices and briefing rooms like? Are they modern and equipped with good lighting and furnishings? This is where you'll be undertaking your all-important briefings and sitting exams, so you want a sound learning environment.

People.

Behind every good flying school are good people. What is the sense of the school when you first walk in? Are the instructors professionally dressed and polite, or do they look like they're auditioning for 'Top Gun 2', and you're kind of in the way? Is there a mix of junior instructors and senior instructors, or just a few youngsters starting out? Personally, I have found some brand-new instructors amongst the most dedicated and proficient in the early phases, but they still need mentoring from the old hands. Equally important is a spread of experience so that you are not kept waiting for a senior instructor to check you as you reach the various tests and milestones. Furthermore, to train for a commercial licence, ideally, the instructor should have some commercial experience beyond the world of flight instruction.

Take the time to speak with the Chief Flying Instructor. If the CFI doesn't have time to speak with you on that first day, then make a booking to chat when it's convenient. If this proves difficult, or impossible, then that isn't a good indicator at a very early stage. I have been a CFI and it can be a very demanding job, but a CFI is also part of the management team and should actively assist a new prospective customer.

What is the support staff situation? What do other students think of the school? Is there a full-time receptionist attending to the front desk and enquiries, or are bookings and new clients rated as a secondary duty for the flying instructors? Interestingly, in my experience, I have found that a common feature of good flying schools is a dedicated staff member attending to the front office duties.

Files and Flying.

Ask to see a copy of a training file. Does it look professionally presented, or has the same master file been photocopied for the last twenty years with no thought of re-visiting the syllabus and making it better? Perhaps they are of a new digital, online format. Also, have a look at the training notes provided by the school for apparent quality. While you won't necessarily appreciate the content at this point, if their briefing notes are poorly presented, not readily at hand, or worse, don't exist at all then this is critical as these notes are the link between the text-book and how the flying school executes the lesson in the air. If they just recommend you purchase a manual and self-study, then that isn't what you're looking for.

The way in which a school administers its ground-based responsibilities often reflects how they operate in the skies. If attention to the paperwork is poor, then you'll probably find that it is one of those schools that just want you in the aeroplane, ticking over the meter and then out the door as soon as you've paid. Flight training is a broader-based undertaking than that; the flight time is critical, but its quality is dependent upon many supporting factors outside the cockpit.

Longevity.

Is the school well established with a reputation that precedes it? If so, they are probably doing something right as longevity in itself is difficult in the flight training business. I say "probably" because some sharks have been known to live for over seventy years. Hence, the recommendation of past and present students can be invaluable third-party information. Bear in mind that a newly established school may also have much to offer; new aeroplanes, unbridled enthusiasm and a desperate need to grow its customer base. They may have poached experienced instructors to provide the expertise and be situated in a new building where the paint has just dried.

Longevity should be considered with all prospective schools. Does the operation look like it's running on a shoe-string and won't be here in a year? (Sometimes the big, glossy schools suffer from this too). As such, a word of warning, never put large amounts of cash up front for your training. I have seen more than one school close its doors and leave its students thousands of dollars out of pocket. Pay promptly following each lesson, or you may choose to deposit a small amount into an account for ease of payment, but don't be talked into depositing a whole lot up front.

Cost.

The biggest variable and most critical factor for many is simply the cost. Flight training is not an inexpensive exercise, and anyone who tries to tell you otherwise is kidding themselves. As with so many things, you'll get what you pay for. Better aeroplanes will come at a premium above their clapped-out counterparts. Some schools may charge for briefings, but that is more cost efficient than not receiving them and having to repeat flight lessons.

There is all manner of costs associated with flying from equipment to text-books. Ask the school at the outset, what you need to purchase and what they provide. What is the price of these ancillary items? Do they provide ground theory training and at what price? What are the hire rates for the aeroplane and is there an additional fee for flight tests, or a lower rate for solo flying? Ask them REALISTICALLY how many hours it generally takes a student to achieve the licence you're pursuing. What is the breakdown of hours in terms of dual, solo, and tests and what is an estimate of the overall cost? Ascertain this figure before you even start and then add on a little to factor in rising prices and hiccups along the way. As I said, it won't be cheap, but you ultimately get what you pay for.

Learning to fly is a major step, so don't rush in. Take the time to gather information and ask the right questions of the right people. If the answers are muddled or slow in coming, then that's probably a 'red flag' for how they conduct their business. Quality flying schools don't hide their costs or information, and they'll take the time to discuss both with you.

So, there are some tips to set out on your great adventure of flight. It may seem daunting, but it will be well worth it. As I said earlier, these questions are a guide, not a complete answer to all circumstances but they should set you on the right path.
Safe flying!

Points to Remember.

* Consider your flying goals and research which school best suits your individual needs.
* Observe the condition and state of the school premises and aircraft.
* Avoid, if possible, laying down large sums of money 'up front'. Flying schools have been known to go bankrupt.
* Do your research as this may well save you time and money in the long run.

CHAPTER TWO

BE PREPARED

For two simple words, the Boy Scouts motto of 'Be Prepared' has cast its net far and wide. Whether it is an academic endeavour or sporting pursuit, the ability to turn up cold and expect success has been shown to border on folly. Aviation is no exception and it is often the work outside the cockpit that will determine the success within.

Poor Preparation results in Poor Performance.

The term 'Private Pilot' is often misunderstood. The inference that it is almost in opposition to professional aviators is both unfair and inaccurate. Whilst some may choose to aviate for leisure, it is very difficult to be a leisurely aviator. The level of theoretical and practical knowledge required to gain the licence is not insignificant, nor is the ongoing effort and cost to maintain standards and currency.

Regardless of the level of licence, there are regulatory requirements and minimum standards of competency that must be met. There are ongoing check rides and exams, medicals and manuals. This continual scrutiny of the pilot's knowledge and ability is not necessarily the most enjoyable aspect of aviation, but the challenge that stems from it reinforces that flight is a worthy pastime. It's not easy, but very few worthwhile endeavours are.

This scrutiny does not always come from a 'higher authority'; in fact, it most frequently results from the standards we impose upon ourselves. Much of the ability to meet these challenges will not be found in the cockpit, but in the time spent considering a flight's conduct before the engine even starts. Sound flying begins with sound preparation.

The old adage goes that "poor preparation results in poor performance". Ask any Flight Examiner about the warning signs of a poorly prepared candidate and they will be able to recount several instances where the outcome of the test was obvious even before taking flight. A pilot may have wonderful manipulative skills, but these will very quickly be undermined by a lack of preparation, organisation and attitude.

Incomplete paperwork, poor punctuality, scruffy appearance, absent equipment and inadequate briefing materials are just some of the 'red flags' of a pilot who is struggling to perform. The majority are tasks that could have been completed well in advance of the flight and free of the pressure imposed by time constraints. Yet time and again, pilots will box themselves into stress-filled corners because of lack of preparation.

While these warning signs may be evident to an examiner or flight instructor, it is even more critical that they serve as warnings signs to the individual. They may indicate that today might not be the day to go flying, or if it is, that a little extra vigilance is needed after a few long deep breaths. From time to time everyone will run late or forget to pack a chart in their 'nav bag', but it is important that these are not symptoms of poor overall preparation.

A Personal Preflight.

So why can't we just get in and go without adequate preparation?

Primarily, aviation is a task that calls for thorough planning. It requires the co-ordination of numerous tasks while being subject to the variables of weather, clearances and aircraft serviceability to name just a few. When these variables compound with time constraints and the everyday demands of operating an aircraft, the pressure can begin to mount. The cockpit can very quickly escalate to a place of spiralling workload at the expense of the fundamental safety of the aircraft and those on board.

As humans, we are only endowed with a finite brain capacity to manage multiple tasks; there are only so many balls that we can keep in the air. If the workload is permitted to intensify beyond our limits, the ability to prioritise and make decisions will be compromised. We may become myopic and fixate on a single task at the expense of the overall conduct and safety of the flight. Hence, it is imperative that we have a strategy in place for the management of the workload and one of the greatest means of achieving this is through sound preflight preparation. Many of the tasks that can prove distracting can be addressed before the chocks are ever pulled away, it just requires thinking ahead.

Thinking ahead can take many forms and placed under the banner of 'preflight preparation'. Firstly, there are core qualities that are expected of a licensed pilot. These include a sound knowledge of the aircraft, its performance, limitations and systems. Not just an aircraft type exam that was passed at the time of endorsement, but a practical understanding of the aircraft that is reviewed from time to time. Similarly, the rules and regulations that will govern the flight should be fundamental knowledge.

Ensuring that all licences and ratings are up to date is a basic responsibility, but equally critical is the matter of flying currency. Currency can be precisely defined by regulations, but these must be seen for what they are; base-level requirements. Only you know if you are satisfied with your level of currency and comfortable to strap loved ones into the seats behind you. Are you clear on your engine failure procedures? How long since you last flew a go-around? There is legally current and genuinely current; ensure the latter is always the case.

Personal fitness is also too often overlooked. Head colds and blocked ears are an obvious indicator of not being fit to fly, but it is the more subtle issues that can sometimes slip beneath the radar. Inadequate or restless sleep, pressures at home or the office can impinge upon a pilot's performance without manifesting in the form of straightforward symptoms. These silent ailments are no less threatening to flight safety than their diseased counterparts are.

Whether it is our knowledge, currency or fitness in question, we need to be able to step away and logically assess whether we are up to the task of flying. If there is *any* doubt, our responsibility is to not go flying. As such, these assessments are best made well before the flight as there is added pressure when we stand at the airport with the aircraft on the ramp and our passengers waiting expectantly. The earlier we assess our readiness, the more time there is to rectify the situation.

A State of Readiness.

In addition to self-assessing the fundamental issues of readiness, there are numerous common-sense preflight strategies to ensure that the flight goes as smoothly as possible.

At the forefront is time management. Anything that can be calculated, organised, studied, flight planned, booked or dismissed *before* arriving at the airfield is an opportunity to alleviate the load on the day you go flying. Additionally, by attending to these matters well in advance permits the exercise to be unrushed. A review of the weather or NOTAMS the night before may avoid surprises and offer time to plan alternative strategies. Time is critical and very few sound decisions are made in haste. This theme carries through to the day of the flight. Allow for bad traffic driving to the airport, allow additional time for flight planning and readying the aircraft. A pilot shouldn't be racing around or their body will be seated in the cockpit with their mind still at the briefing office.

'Armchair flying' is another technique to fine tune flight management away from the aeroplane. Aerobatic pilots can be seen, standing alone, arms out and 'flying' their routine through their mind's eye. For emergency drills, envisaging scenarios before they eventuate can reduce the shock value and potential confusion that may result from an event such as an engine failure. Reviewing the vital actions in the comfort of your home and re-briefing them before take-off will go a long way to providing clarity of thought and executing the appropriate actions should the unexpected occur. Airline pilots frequently armchair fly 'engine out' manoeuvres or other emergency procedures, particularly as they prepare for simulator check rides. The same benefits are there for all pilots in rehearsing procedures to the point that they become second nature. Again, this frees up some of that finite 'brain space'.

Cockpit organisation is also too often overlooked. Ensuring that ALL of the charts are on hand, along with licences, pens, flight plans and the like can be done well before departure time. Devise a system where the same items are stored in the same compartments of the flight bag, thus not only highlighting any absences but also permitting blind access on a cold, wet night in turbulence. The same applies to stowage in the cockpit; item must be secure and accessible. If you drop a pencil, have another, have your charts folded and ready to go at your fingertips. Flight decks are not for foraging.

Always beware of unsecured items great and small. I know of one instance where a loose coin brought an aircraft down when it became wedged at the base of the control column. The instructor was a decorated World War Two 'Dambuster' pilot, but without full control, the deHavilland Chipmunk crashed killing both on board. An absolute tragedy on so many levels.

Whatever the preflight strategy may be, simply having one puts the pilot ahead of the game. There will always be instances of last minute changes and the best laid plans going awry, but being timely and organised will even offset some of this drama. Even so, do not permit yourself to be rushed or pushed into a corner beyond your zone of comfort and competency. As every preflight moves towards taking flight, as a final check, the pilot should ask, "Am I ready?" If the answer is "no", it is never too late to walk away in the interests of safety.

Be Prepared.

Whether flying professionally or for leisure, there will always be responsibilities and duties requiring attention. With equal certainty, at the heart of flying for every pilot, there should be a great degree of enjoyment.

To ensure that this occurs, pilots need to eradicate as many pressures and stresses as they possibly can well in advance of taking to the air. A sound approach to preflight preparation and the development of personal strategies and organisation will go a long way to meeting these goals. With as many issues addressed as possible, it will free up mental capacity to cater for unexpected eventualities and manage the flight with a minimum of stress and also allow some gazing beyond the cumulus and the contours below. After all, we have the best seat in the house.

Points to Remember.

* We may choose to aviate for leisure, but it is very difficult to be a leisurely aviator.

* Many of the tasks that can prove distracting in flight can be addressed before flight.

* There is legally current and genuinely current; ensure the latter is always the case.

* Cockpit organisation is too often overlooked.

* As a final check, a pilot should ask, "Am I ready?" If the answer is "no", it is never too late to walk away in the interests of safety.

CHAPTER THREE

TAKING FLIGHT

With so much emphasis on the approach and landing phase of flight and the quest for a smooth touchdown, the humble take-off is frequently overlooked. Often perceived as simply lining up, pushing the levers forward and pulling back when the time is right, the take-off is actually a very critical phase of each and every flight.

Surface to Air.

There is nothing quite like that moment when the earth falls away from the wheels and the earthbound restraints transition into freedom in all three dimensions. From the initial surge of power to the nose pointing skyward, guiding the rest of the aircraft towards its natural habitat; this is when flight becomes a reality. This is the take-off and for all its majesty, it is also a potentially vulnerable time.

Like landing, it is a manoeuvre conducted at ground level where there is little time and altitude for forgiveness. It is susceptible to all manner of variables; environmental, aerodynamic and human in origin. Accordingly, like any phase of flight, the take-off should be given the respect and consideration it deserves. Attempts to rush it can at least result in poor handling and at worst leave the aircraft exposed to all manner of lethal variables.

Fundamentally, aircraft are not designed for ground operations, they are meant to fly. As such, designers endeavour to build an undercarriage that will sustain the impact of landing, maintain a straight line at high speed, taxi at slow speeds and offer up the lowest possible weight penalty in the process. Similarly, the wing is meant to fly and generally fly fast. For the majority of designs, the slow speed envelope is recognised as a necessary evil in transitioning the aeroplane to and from flight, so often aerodynamic devices on the leading and trailing edges are added to facilitate this. As such, on take-off, the undercarriage will be asked to absorb the shock and slipperiness of all manner of surfaces as we reconfigure the wing so it will fly at speeds that it would really prefer not to.

At the helm sits the pilot who has hopefully both configured the aircraft correctly and considered an array of possible eventualities. Should the take-off go awry, decisions will need to be made in a split second and yet enacted with precision. As with so many aspects of aviation, the result of thorough preparation is often a routine non-event. Take-offs are no exception to this rule.

The Goal.

In its most basic form, the purpose of the take-off is to transition the aircraft safely from the ground into the air. It is not to be thought of purely as the instant of lift-off, for there are several components of the take-off both preceding this moment and following it. In fact, the take-off can be considered as commencing with its planning in terms of weight and balance, performance data and the ambient conditions. Likewise, the take-off can be thought of becoming a 'climb' only when the aircraft is reconfigured and at a safe altitude. This may involve reducing power and the retraction of flaps and undercarriage, or simply extinguishing lights and selecting the fuel pump off; it will vary from type to type and even departure to departure.

The take-off is virtually a 'blink' in the overall duration of a flight. However, the degree of preparation isn't a function of time; just ask any Olympic sprinter or world class photographer. Safely executing a take-off is a combination of consideration and physical execution and both should be treated with equal respect. To start, let's review what is actually involved in taking our aircraft from the runway to the sky.

A Numbers Game.

Before the park brake is even released, the ability of the aircraft to physically perform the take-off manoeuvre must be checked. This is a function of numerous factors including aircraft weight, payload, centre of gravity, the runway environment and ambient conditions. Each of these variables plays a significant role in their own way and to overlook a lone aspect can be fraught with danger.

In most cases, the aircraft's approved Flight Manual is the defining document in matters of performance. Some larger operators may have an entire approved loading system that is a stand-alone manual or in modern times, part of the Electronic Flight Bag. Whatever the means, there is always a valid method to calculate the limits of aircraft performance in executing a take-off.

The aircraft must be able to accelerate and climb away at a safe speed with adequate obstacle clearance in the distance available. In the case of multi-engine aircraft there will also be a need to climb away if one engine fails on take-off. In higher category aircraft, the 'stop-go' and other scenarios, become a performance dictator. Fortunately, the hard work has been done by test pilots and performance engineers when the aircraft is certified, so the preflight process is a case of arithmetic gymnastics rather than 'trial and error' destructive testing off the end of the runway.

Typically, with most small piston powered aeroplanes, the number of seats doesn't directly reflect everyday uplift of the aircraft. You may well *plan* to take 4 people aloft in a Piper Cherokee 140, but that will rule out anything near full fuel tanks. To this end, performance calculations often require the pilot to make do with the best permissible solution. If a full load of passengers is a requirement on a cross country flight, the fuel load may need to be reduced and additional refuelling stops must be planned. The equation will be a combination of aircraft weight, payload, people and fuel without exceeding any limits. If the numbers don't add up then it might be time to consider upgrading to a larger, more powerful aeroplane to meet your needs.

Further complicating the matter is that even if the total weight to be uplifted is legal, it must also be loaded in a manner that the aircraft remains 'balanced'. Like a see-saw, the aircraft can tend to pitch nose up or down depending on how the aircraft is loaded in relation to its centre of gravity. Too far forward and the nose may not want to lift off on take-off, too far to the rear and the nose may just keeping pitching skyward after rotation until the aircraft stalls. To avoid the balance of the aircraft leading to disastrous controllability issues, a graphical representation or tabular calculation of the limits fore and aft is used. Calculations of load distribution must have the weight and balance of the aeroplane falling within the safe region known as the Centre of Gravity 'envelope'. Bearing in mind that this position may also change enroute as fuel is burned.

I lost a friend to this very issue when his aircraft was loaded with an aft Centre of Gravity. As he burned off fuel the CofG moved further and further to the rear, although he was unaware of the fact as his autopilot was engaged. Ultimately the autopilot could no longer cope and when it disengaged suddenly, the now unstable aircraft flew a series of ever-increasing oscillations until the aircraft impacted the ground killing all on board. It was a dark night and it must have been terrifying. Possibly if the problem had been recognised, the rearmost passengers could have crawled forward to return the status quo. But that is very easy for me to say in hindsight from the comfort of my office. The thought of that accident still saddens me today.

So your aircraft is now loaded to below its maximum limit with fuel, folks and freight distributed in a balanced manner. The next piece of the puzzle relates to the runway environment. Is it long enough? Is the surface covered in long, wet grass which will impede acceleration? Is it sloping uphill? What is the current temperature and prevailing winds? These considerations must also be assessed using the performance charts in verifying that the available runway is suitable for take-off.

Only when the aircraft performance data has been calculated with respect to weight and balance and airfield limitations can a take-off be legally and safely executed. Accident investigations are littered with instances where pilots either overlooked or chose to ignore the performance envelopes of their aircraft. Take the time to do the numbers and peace of mind and safety will inevitably follow.

Ready?

For many of us, the hardest part of the day is opening our eyes, throwing our legs over the side of the bed and starting the day. Our mind hasn't quite snapped out of its slumber and our bodies are not yet fully prepared for motion. It won't take much to get going, but there is that short lag in the lead up to the day. For an aircraft, leaping into the sky is not too dissimilar.

As the aircraft sits in the run-up bay, it may only be minutes since we have 'woken it up'. Its temperatures and pressures may be sitting in the lower bands of the dials and its trim setting, flaps and fuel selections may be left over from the night before. It would be pointless and foolhardy to open the throttles in this state and expect with full assurance that the aircraft will perform soundly and safely take us aloft. To this end, the pre take-off sequences are a vital aspect of flight.

Every company and individual will have their own order of events; just as long as there is an order. It will comprise of such components as checklists, engine run-ups and briefing to ensure that pilot and aeroplane are both ready for the flight ahead and in particular the critical take-off manoeuvre that is now imminent. It is important not to rush this process as too often a simple oversight of fuel selection, an unsecured seat or incorrect flap setting has brought an otherwise serviceable aeroplane to grief.

This is the last point where the security of the earth still offers limitless options in a comfortable environment. Use the pre take-off sequences, and a short pause afterwards, to ensure that you are absolutely satisfied that all issues have been addressed prior to take-off. It is often said that it is better to be on the ground wishing that you were in the air, than the other way around. Take a moment prior to each take-off to remember this.

With all bases covered and a serviceable aeroplane ready to go, it's time to take flight.

Straight Up.

From the parking bay to the holding point, cast one eye to the sky to gain an appreciation of the traffic situation, local weather and anything of interest such as flocks of birds. Confirm that the windsock reflects what you have planned upon and how it may affect your take-off. In other words, start gaining a deeper appreciation of the airborne environment that you are about to launch into.

THE PRACTICAL PILOT

Even with a clearance at a controlled airport, take a good look in both directions before lining up as even Air Traffic Controllers and other pilots can make mistakes. Having attended to the housekeeping of external lights, switching on the transponder and verifying that you are on the correct runway, the aircraft is now lined up on the centre-line. It only awaits the actions that will convert it from an earthbound misfit to a gravity defying machine.

Everything about the take-off should be smooth. From the gradual advancement of power, to directional control and rotation, there should be a degree of ease in every motion. This is not only sound aircraft handling, but offers a greater opportunity to detect any abnormalities that may arise. While the eyes are predominantly outside, there is a brief scan to the engine instruments to check for normal indications and to the RPM to confirm that the required power is being produced. For turbocharged engines, there is always the potential for an 'over boost' situation as well. When all is confirmed to be in order, the scan inside should mainly be seeking the critical speeds as the take-off develops.

If you routinely fly the same aeroplane, there may be a gross error check of how much time or how far down the runway it takes to accelerate to a certain speed. This can provide an early warning to a poorly performing engine or a significantly contaminated runway surface.

The Take-Off Safety Speed (TOSS) provides a margin over the stall speed and is a minimum speed for lifting off and flying away safely. It may differ from the recommended lift off speed at which the pilot rotates the aircraft into the air, but is always worth committing to memory as a critical speed. Coaxing an aircraft into the air prematurely can leave an aircraft 'mushing' along in ground effect with no chance of actually climbing away. Furthermore, it cannot be emphasised enough to follow the manufacturer's recommended take-off technique as each aircraft type can have their own idiosyncrasies.

The actual rotation of the aircraft into the air should be smooth and is often quoted as being around 3 degrees per second. Whatever the rate is, the aircraft should not be 'yanked' abruptly into the air as this introduces a series of potential issues from tail-strikes to over-rotation and the bleeding of speed at a critical time. Eased into the air at the correct speed, the take-off will provide the aircraft with the best available performance. In real terms this equates to safety margins on minimum speeds and optimum obstacle clearance at the far end. From there the task involves establishing a safe climb-out and configuring the aeroplane for departure.

What's the Hurry?

Once airborne, the job is far from over. Vigilance remains an important task and should be spread between flying the aircraft accurately, monitoring aircraft performance, looking out for traffic and being at the ready for the dreaded engine failure after take-off. By virtue of this, the pilot on 'climb out' is quite occupied and the workload is high. Throw into the mix a radio transmission or two at an unfamiliar airfield and it can become downright busy.

To this end, there is no hurry to attend to secondary tasks. Jet airliners normally climb to 1,000 feet before they consider reducing power and this isn't a bad policy when the aircraft is equipped with prop levers either. Why hurriedly turn off auxiliary fuel pumps or retract the take-off flaps unless there is a chance of exceeding their extension speed? Climb the aircraft away from the ground and then begin converting it into the cruise-climb.

There would undoubtedly be a great deal of regret if the wrong switch was actioned or an actual failure took place as the fuel boost pump was flicked off at 300'. After all, it is there to back up the engine driven pump in critical phases and normally, if the engine genuinely fails, one of the first actions is to switch it on. So just leave it alone. And that is not to mention the fact that locating and actioning switches draws the eyes inside the cockpit when they should either be outside or focused on an instrument scan if in IMC.

In a similar fashion, when a light aircraft with a retractable undercarriage takes off at a major airport with 3,500 metres of runway, there's no urgency to retract the undercarriage. If the engine stops, you're landing ahead so you may as well already have the gear out and not sweat on it extending in time in an emergency. A number of pilots call "runway away, gear away" as the upwind threshold disappears under the nose.

Like the take-off roll and rotation, the climb out and re-configuration should be done with method and forethought, not haste. Consider the variables well before you advance the throttles and the departure will unfold far more smoothly. Aircraft should be flown and not merely pushed around without giving consideration to handling and consequences. It is just one area of airmanship that separates flight from so many other activities.

Taking Flight.

The take-off is a relatively simple manoeuvre which constitutes a critical phase of flight. It is one of those aspects of aircraft handling that is easy to do, but easy to do badly. What will further compound the challenge are the seemingly endless variables that can impact upon the take-off sequence. However, that's another chapter, all of its own.

Points to Remember.

* The take-off is virtually a 'blink' in the overall duration of a flight but its importance must not be overlooked.

* Understand and apply the take-off limitations as they apply to your aircraft.

* Ensure that both the pilot and the aircraft are fully prepared for the take-off. If not, do not proceed and rectify the issue from the safety of the earth.

* Once airborne, continue to focus on the take-off. Do not rush into any subsequent procedures.

CHAPTER FOUR

TROUBLES ON TAKE-OFF

There are variables outside of the pilot's hands that nevertheless must be considered and countered to ensure a safe take-off. From environmental effects to emergencies, we need to consider subtle safety strategies to manage these differing conditions and appreciate that there is more than one way to take flight.

The Powers That Be.

Whether man takes to the land, seas or skies he will always be at the mercy of the elements to some degree. They can be seen as a threat or a challenge, but either way nature is an inescapable component of aviation. From crosswinds and climate to wet runways and windshear, the range of conditions are as diverse as the planet itself.

There will be days when those conditions exceed the performance of the aeroplane or our own level of skill and the prudent choice in these situations is to stay on the ground and fly another day. However, more frequently the elements will be within the grasp of both crew and machine, so due consideration should be given before advancing the levers and accelerating down the runway.

The wind can be our friend when it is blowing straight onto our nose for take-off. Reducing the distance of the ground roll and increasing the angle of climb and obstacle clearance, a headwind is the ideal ally provided by nature. Unfortunately, pressure systems, noise abatement procedures and local topography do not always ensure that the wind direction is our friend. At times it will blow from abeam and present a challenging crosswind, while a wind from behind will penalise performance in the opposite manner that a headwind can aid it. Tailwinds will both extend the ground roll and erode the angle of climb. To this end it is critical that take-off performance charts are consulted regarding the take-off distance required with a tailwind, while the aircraft limitations will generally state a maximum tailwind component regardless of the amount of available runway.

The major consideration in the event of a crosswind is the issue of directional control. The 'downwind' wing is shielded by the fuselage to a degree, while conversely the 'upwind' wing is in receipt of greater air flow, encouraging it to fly. Consequently, the upwind wing needs to be held on the runway during the take-off roll with the appropriate use of aileron. Compounding this directional issue is the effect of the crosswind on the aircraft's fuselage and the tendency for the aeroplane to 'weather-cock' into wind. Through a combination of control inputs, which may actually see rudder and aileron in opposition, the goal is to maintain that centre-line during the take-off roll. Once airborne, the aim is to smoothly return the controls to the balanced inputs required for the climb out as the aircraft is now free to weather-cock into wind. The next challenge is to fly the extended centreline without being blown downwind. Sounds like fun?

Temperature is another environmental consideration for the take-off. Warmer temperatures can be detrimental to the take-off on a number of counts. Firstly, the heated air is less dense and stifles the performance of the aerofoil to lift the aircraft from the runway. So much so, that for every degree Celsius above 15 degrees at sea level, it is equivalent to raising the airfield a further 120 feet above sea level. For instance, a 30-degree day would equate to an airfield at 1800' higher than its true elevation. Further to this, the propeller is less efficient in the thinner air and the engine suffers from reduced volumetric efficiency with a corresponding drop in power output. All of this equates to a longer ground run and reduced climb performance and once again this needs to be verified preflight in the aircraft's performance manuals. With humidity also affecting air density and take-off performance, the old catch-cry to be wary when conditions are "Hot, High or Humid" makes very good sense.

Conversely, cold climates may equate to better Take-off performance due to their positive effect on air density. In these regions, the greater threat lies in the presence of frost, ice or snow. These forms of moisture can severely destroy the lift characteristics of an aerofoil, so as always a thorough preflight of the aircraft is essential, with increased vigilance towards contaminated surfaces. Furthermore, when present upon the runway, visible moisture may not only retard the take-off acceleration and impede directional control, but it risks being ingested into engines.

The surface does not need to be contaminated by water, ice or snow to hamper the take-off roll. Sometimes it is the natural surface of the runway that proves to be an effective retardant in the form of long grass or desert sands. Obviously, the presence of water will compound the issue, but unkempt grass can provide quite a surprise to the student pilot raised solely on black asphalt and painted centre-lines. Sometimes the Flight Manual will recommend a 'soft field' technique which advocates the use of a higher flap setting to allow the aircraft to become airborne at a lesser speed. However, the penalty comes after take-off when the climb performance may be degraded by the extended flap, so ensure that obstacle clearance is not a particular issue.

The good news is that environmental factors have been around since the Wright Brothers and much has been learnt in the years in between. Consequently, aircraft performance manuals cater for most situations and if you abide by the book figures, you should be covered. If the prevailing conditions are so unique that they are not catered or they exceed the published limits, then the only safe option is to stay on the ground and wait for conditions to improve.

The Big Bang. (...and sometimes not)

An engine failure on take-off is regarded as one of the most critical situations a pilot can encounter. In a single-engined aircraft, gravity and inertia become the powerplant and only limited options and time lie ahead. In a multi-engine aircraft, the outlook may be more promising if the failed engine can be secured and the aircraft is able to fly away to a safe altitude. I emphasise 'may' as only the foolhardy believe that a light twin's second engine is always a guarantee of climb performance.

Whether in a single or a twin, an 'escape plan' should be formulated in the event of an engine failure. What is the terrain situation on upwind? Are there parallel runway operations? Are there forced landing fields or a nearby airport? If I am struggling to maintain height in a twin, at what height will I start to turn back towards the field and will I turn left or right? Clarifying these issues prior to take-off is invaluable and may in fact dictate your departure plan with everything working. An early or delayed crosswind turn in a single may avoid some nasty terrain should the engine go silent. Better safe than sorry.

Furthermore, it would be remiss to consider engine failures without remembering that they are not always a cut and dried 'bang' followed by silence. I have had instances in both light aircraft and airliners where the failure was only 'partial'. In the Cessna 210 a cylinder had failed in the cruise and in the Boeing 737 we had ingested a bird on take-off. In both instances, there was an initial 'bang', but the engine continued to provide valuable power and performance associated with only mild vibration. I was fortunate in both cases.

It may only be a partial failure, or even sound a whole lot worse than it is. The repeat offenders of a blown tyre on take-off or a seat belt outside the door banging on the fuselage have both led pilots to believe that the aircraft engine was about to self-destruct. No matter how much noise or vibration may be present, verify the aircraft performance. If the aircraft is till performing satisfactorily, don't rush into anything, but keep climbing for precious altitude where you have options and time to carefully analyse the problem.

To Go or Not to Go?

Airline category aircraft have specific data relating to the point at which a take-off can be safely continued in the case of an engine failure. Similarly, beyond a certain speed, the decision to reject a take-off and remain on the ground exposes the aircraft to the real danger of over-running the runway. While the decision to go, or not to go, may be straightforward for such things as an engine failure in a Cessna 152, matters are not always so black and white.

Light aircraft don't generally possess a "go or no-go" speed, but there are incidents that may take place on the take-off roll that are not necessarily an emergency, but will require attention at some point. The challenge then is to ascertain what action will present the greatest risk; continuing to fly or over-running the runway. Each decision will be different for each pilot, runway and aircraft and even the stage of the take-off. However, it is worth dedicating some thought to the scenarios before they ever occur.

One of the most common incidents is a door coming open just upon rotation on take-off. For all the associated noise of rushing air and startled passengers, generally the door will only pop open a small amount and be kept quite flush by the relative airflow. On a 3,000 metre international runway, you may decide to re-land ahead, but on a short remote dirt airstrip with a precipitous drop off the far end, you may decide to continue the take-off. Additionally, the point of decision may be indicated by a physical feature along the runway indicating the distance remaining, or may be as simple as being airborne is the cue to continue. Each day will be different, but a plan in advance is well worth having.

A door opening is just one such scenario. Poor acceleration on the take-off roll, a realisation of an incorrect flap setting or a seat sliding back prior to lift-off are all events that are best considered before they strike. The very best technique is to guard against such eventualities with good airmanship and sound checklist discipline.

Taken for Granted.

In many ways, the take-off manoeuvre is a straightforward exercise of aircraft control. However, there are ample opportunities for this critical phase of flight to turn sour. The seat belt hanging out of the aeroplane and doors popping open on take-off have both been quoted as distracting occurrences on take-off. Wrong trim settings, incorrect flap selection and an unsecured seat sliding back are potentially fatal oversights in the take-off process. A misidentification of the correct runway has seen a number of accidents occur, particularly in low visibility situations, while fatal accidents have stemmed from attempted take-offs on occupied runways. Who can forget the collision of the KLM and Pan Am 747s at Tenerife in 1977 that stemmed from confusion on the flight deck and poor visibility.

Our best defence is often in our own hands. Respect the performance limitations of the aeroplane, follow standard operating procedures and conduct checklists in a thorough, measured manner. Even so, there are additional 'safety filters' we can introduce to our flying; the engine out scenario and departure planning are two examples. Prior to lining up, we can verify that we are at the correct holding point before entering the runway. Additionally, a final assessment of the wind, local weather and terrain is timely. Consciously look for aircraft before lining up and be aware of how design features such as a high wing may impede the lookout. Once aligned, our check of the runway direction against the compass is another verification of the runway.

Sometimes, there are final checks that vary from pilot to pilot just before they start the take-off roll. It may be a push back upon the seat to verify that it is absolutely locked in. For others a last look at 'Fuel, Flap and Trim' may be seen as worthwhile. However, once the take-off has commenced, the focus must be purely on the manoeuvre as it has been trained for. If it hasn't been checked now, it's not going to be. If it is that critical, this may be one of the reasons for which you decide to reject the take-off if it is safe to do so.

Taking Flight.

We have said previously that with so much emphasis on the approach and landing phase of flight, the humble take-off is frequently overlooked. Often perceived as simply lining up, pushing the levers forward and pulling back when the time is right, the take-off is actually a very critical phase of each and every flight.

A truly safely executed take-off is one that has catered for a series of events that hopefully never occur. Furthermore, the variables that are presented on each occasion need to be considered for their impact upon the take-off manoeuvre before we start to roll down the runway. Only when man and machine are truly ready should they venture into the sky above. When prepared, the take-off can then safely open the door to taking flight.

Points to Remember.

* Consider the environmental conditions and their potential impact on the take-off.

* Have a plan of action in the event of an engine failure BEFORE you commence the take-off.

* Always consider the possible reasons to reject a take-off and the runway length remaining.

* A truly safely executed take-off is one that has catered for a series of events that hopefully never occur.

CHAPTER FIVE

A MATTER OF COURSE

There is no doubting that GPS has revolutionised the manner in which we transit the globe. For the visual pilot it has brought precision navigation to the cockpit at a highly affordable price. However, in some instances it has also opened the door to an old foe of aviation; complacency.

A Revolution.

When Elrey Jeppesen plotted his way around protruding peaks and wild weather 75 years ago, he set in motion aeronautical charts as we've come to know them today. Decade after decade, the art of navigation has sought further precision and reliability as aircraft have increased in speed, range and capacity while our planet has seemingly shrunk at a similar rate.

The stars upon which the ancient mariners once gazed have been crowded by a sea of man-made satellites skimming across the night sky. From a constellation of these satellites in medium earth orbit, the signals are relayed that permit the calculation of a position down to a matter of metres, or less. And this is not the realm of lunar modules or long haul flight decks, this information can today be found on the dashboards of the family car and mobile phones.

These Global Positioning Systems (GPS) have revolutionised not only the 'how' of navigation, but the 'who'. Precision is at the fingertips of the masses on a moderate budget. For aviators who transit the three dimensions without the comfort of pulling over to the kerb, GPS has proved a blessing. It has also reinforced that in navigation we should look before we leap.

The Hills Are Alive.

It was once said that the only hard thing about aviation is the ground. Whilst a gross over-simplification, there is no denying that controlled flight into terrain (CFIT) has plagued aviation from its earliest days. Perfectly serviceable aircraft have been flown into the ground for all manner of reasons. For visual pilots, often weather has played a major role, forcing pilots down amongst the treetops or diverting them off track as they struggle remain clear of cloud and rain.

In such scenarios, correctly used, GPS is potentially a pilot's greatest ally. The ever-improving moving map displays and terrain overlays offer a greatly enhanced aid to situational awareness. Furthermore, in these high workload situations flailing charts and dropped protractors have been replaced by an accurate, track-oriented display.

So why are the old demons still with us and VFR pilots impacting the terrain?

Obviously the reasons are many, from airmanship issues to planning and enroute decision making. However, one aspect of these tragedies involves GPS. In some cases, this great advance in navigation can actually reduce the level of a pilot's situational awareness and lead to fixation and dependency. This is not the fault of GPS, rather the way that we as pilots interface with it.

A Double-Edged Sword.

Visual navigation has always been a challenging aspect of aviation and consequently one of the most satisfying. At the mercy of the invisible wind and the seasonal changing of terrain, the picture can look significantly different from 500 feet to 5000 feet. These variables must always be factored into the mathematics of speed, heading and time. Consequently, this form of navigation is often thought of as an art as well as a science.

GPS has increased the science by offering not only precise position information, but direct tracking and so much more at the touch of a button. For some, the ease at which these numerous functions can be achieved has come at the cost of their basic navigation skills. The art has been replaced by a dependence upon technology.

In navigation, straight lines are preferable, right? The shortest distance equates to reduced flight times and savings through reduced fuel burn and engine wear. In truth, the answer is both yes and no. It is true that straight lines are more efficient, but airmanship encompasses so much more than pure numbers. Direct tracks do not always consider terrain, freezing levels or airspace organisation.

Where possible, visual flight routes have traditionally been planned to permit the confirmation of an aircraft's position and progress by reference to ground based features. By default, these features have generally equated to better terrain. Roads and rail lines have sought to wind their way around particularly rugged country due to ease of construction. Towns have subsequently grown along these thoroughfares and waterways, all of which offer aids to the task of map reading.

Such waypoints offer more than merely a visual fix of one's position. They prompt a cycle of cockpit management that encompasses many elements, including fuel management, time-keeping, compass alignment, log-keeping, chart organisation and so on. Without these waypoints, it requires a different skill set and self-discipline to avoid motorway-style, cruise control and white line fever. Just set and forget.

The direct line "go to" function bypasses these waypoints and can stretch the sector length and consequently the time between any cycle of cockpit organisation. It can increase the period between radio calls and seduce single engine pilots over inhospitable terrain where their options are limited should the engine go silent. Even with a serviceable aircraft, rising hills can reduce the corridor beneath cloud and add a further risk factor should the visibility drop and a 180-degree turn be called for. Even for flight in instrument conditions, the straight line can lead to higher Lowest Safe Altitudes or LSALTs, and lower freezing levels.

In fact, the apparent ease of GPS begs its use beyond its purpose. Some misguided pilots will 'design' their own instrument approach into their home port and fly unpublished approaches. Obviously these unsurveyed 'approaches' do not account for terrain in the splay, loss of an engine and adequate missed approach tolerances. Additionally, unqualified pilots have been caught out flying legitimate GPS approaches. Whilst this has also occurred in the past, the complexity of non-precision approaches has provided a hurdle in many cases. GPS offers seemingly straight-in, runway aligned approaches to one and all at the touch of a button.

Even the 'touch of a button' can prove to be a trap. Visual flight calls for the vast majority of the pilot's scan to be outside the cockpit. Impressive map displays and the need for data input drag that focus back into the cockpit and the expense of lookout. It leads to the pilot becoming 'head down' in a visual environment with increased risk of collision and reduced awareness of the surrounding terrain and potential forced landing fields.

It is a problem not limited to the VFR pilot. The rapid growth of technology in all areas of aviation has brought a new set of problems as humans interface with computers. Even the pilots in multi-crew jets are prone to fixation and vulnerable to the errors of push-button data entry. The difference being that they often have rigid procedures in place to provide cross-checking and restricting 'heads down' operation in the terminal area. The single pilot doesn't have this benefit.

The list of potential traps of GPS can go on. However, the benefits of the system undoubtedly outweigh these. It is the management of GPS, not the tool itself that generates the risks. GPS needs to be integrated into the visual pilot's navigation toolbox; it is not designed to replace it.

Making it Work.

Used properly, GPS is the greatest aid to navigation available to the VFR pilot. It can provide a wealth of information at a moment's notice. However, it needs to become part of the pilot's overall navigation strategy, from pre-flight planning to post-flight review. Cross-checked and re-confirmed with the healthy mistrust that defines the situationally aware pilot.

In the planning phase, airmanship rather than expediency should always remain the determining factor. Even multi-engined airliners in the Flight Levels plan their route within range of alternate airfields in the event of engine failure or depressurisation. Look at potential waypoints enroute, navigable features, airfields and terrain with a view to them assisting your navigation and providing safe alternatives in the event of emergency. It can be surprising how few additional track miles are required to provide a significantly better route over 'forced-landing friendly' terrain.

GPS fits into this planning wonderfully with its ability to create waypoints along your route. Manually calculated tracks and distances can be cross-checked against those generated by the GPS when the waypoints are entered. Consequently, your navigation becomes an effective two-pronged attack in which visual reference and precision GPS complement each other.

Similarly, enroute, the GPS information becomes a component of your cockpit cycle. Time, heading, fuel, track, log are all items that are re-assessed at regular intervals. By referencing the GPS within this cycle, its information can be directly compared to other navigational aspects and assists in avoiding fixation solely on GPS. This fixation can lead to dependency and that is when other supporting forms of navigation can fall away. An old rule is to confirm a landmark by three supporting features, perhaps a town, a rail junction and a river. Applying this to the GPS equipped cockpit, the GPS position can be one of these elements, but you still need to at least see the rail junction and the river.

It must always be remembered that it is *visual* navigation and the eyes remain outside the cockpit most of the time. This is not purely for the purpose of map-reading, but for collision avoidance and the ongoing assessment of weather. Not to mention that outside is where you'll find the scenery too!

Post flight, the GPS generated data can be used to cross-check fuel consumption and what should remain in the tanks. As with the navigational aspects, calculate your long hand figure first so that the GPS figure doesn't lead you to the same outcome by the power of suggestion.

GPS has revolutionised navigation. It has brought even the most basic cockpit blazing into the 21st century via a yoke-mounted moving map. It should always be treated with healthy caution as all interaction with automation must. Take care when entering data by small buttons in a dim cockpit and use gross error checks in advance to confirm the information generated for the pilot. Treat GPS with respect as a component of your navigational array and it will offer tremendous benefits.

Above all, you remain the pilot in command. The GPS is a tool for you to use and not the other way around. By adhering to the sound principles of navigation and airmanship, GPS will allow you to fly with a level of precision and assurance not previously experienced. Arriving overhead, on time and on track will simply be a matter of course.

Points to Remember.

* When possible, plan via navigable features, airfields and terrain with a view to them assisting your navigation and providing safe alternatives in the event of emergency.

* Don't become 'head down' with the task of data entry.

* The GPS is a tool for you to use and not the other way around.

CHAPTER SIX

IN-FLIGHT DIVERSIONS

In aviation, as in life, things do not always go to plan. Despite one's best efforts, intentions and preparation, events can still unfold that call for a change in strategy. When these events take place aloft, pilots need to be able to adapt without undue delay and exercise the options available to them. Under the high workload environment of the cockpit, there is a certain skill set required to successfully execute an in-flight diversion.

Be Ready for Anything.

I once diverted to an alternate airport in an airliner as the weather at the destination had deteriorated rapidly. Only a week earlier, an aircraft had become disabled on the runway, also forcing the thought processes to consider the available options and ready the aircraft to divert elsewhere. In this instance the aircraft was cleared away and our flight arrived as planned, if not as scheduled. Obviously, operating an airline transport category aeroplane has the benefits of auto-pilots, flight management computers (FMC) and multi-crew to alleviate the workload. However, in both cases, it was striking how the principles and considerations of planning these diversions were common to those basic pilot training exercises so very many years ago.

The first thing to consider is that diversions are extremely varied in their nature. Everyone is familiar with the copybook flight-test diversion to the degree that you can almost guess where and when the change in plan will take place. In the real world of the VFR pilot, the case is not always so clear-cut. Deteriorating weather is the traditional foe, while a passenger's worsening health may offer far less warning. An aircraft serviceability issue may call for an expedient landing or a 'wheels up' landing of another aeroplane may take out the only available runway at the destination. Perhaps the diversion is not to a new destination, but a divergence from the planned track to avoid some isolated weather.

As with all aspects of flight, a great deal can be achieved with thorough pre-flight preparation, before the workload of the cockpit has even started. A simple diversion consideration can relate to the destination airfield, should it only be serviced by a single runway. In these cases, it is always worth having the required fuel to reach an alternate airfield as any number of occurrences could render it out of action. For the greater part of the journey, consider the planned route and then expand the perspective to include nearby airports. The level to which this consideration is detailed can be matter of personal choice and available time. At the very least, draw a reasonably sized circle around each airfield as this will enhance situational awareness and offer a ready appreciation of the distance from any particular airport at any particular stage of the flight. Some choose to draw a compass rose on the circle, while others will include basic facts such as elevation, runway direction and radio frequency; it's your choice.

In pre-flight planning, review the weather and NOTAMs for these proximal airports to guard against a well executed diversion to an unavailable airfield. Similarly, consider the location of controlled airspace or active restricted areas in this planning phase. Highlight any significant restrictions in your planning notes so they are at the ready should an in-flight change of plans take place. Also, organise your cockpit, charts, pencils and plans before you depart as this equipment will be needed to be accessed without fuss in flight. Even without concerted effort, these simple measures will begin to formulate an enhanced appreciation of the route you are to fly, which is a definite advantage when the unexpected takes place enroute.

Decisions, Decisions.

Often the most difficult part of the diversion is the initial decision to go elsewhere. The pressure to 'push on' beyond a safe point can often be exacerbated by pride or the desire not to disappoint the passengers. Some folks can tend to procrastinate and continue on aimlessly rather than taking action. Regardless, the safe conduct of the flight rests squarely on the shoulders of the pilot-in-command and any decision must be made in a safe, timely and measured manner.

Firstly, consider why diverting is an option. Is the weather progressively reported as worse than the forecast or is there rising suspicion that the fuel in the tanks will not be enough to arrive safely with reserves? If the facts are enough to cause concern, then there is a reason to consider diverting, getting on the ground and resolving the issue on the safety of Terra Firma. While conservative, an early decision is generally a good decision. Remember that an early radio call to the Flight Service facility is a wise move if the situation, particularly weather, is starting to cause a degree of doubt.

Decisions should be made on the foundation of fact, so gathering all the available information may take some time. It is here that the pre-flight observance of alternate airfields starts to pay dividends in the workload stakes. Consider your options in a measured way, but never ignore flying the aeroplane; it must always remain the first priority. Distraction can pose a real threat in these situations and the flying conditions may already be less than ideal by virtue of the weather closing in and necessitating the diversion. Stay in control, ensure there's adequate fuel in the tanks and maintain safe clearance with the terrain; these are three potential killers that stalk the pilot under pressure.

The speed with which the decision is made may ultimately be determined by the circumstances on the day. A wall of water falling from the heavens ahead, or an incurable rough running engine will call for action without delay. However, if the issue is a disabled aircraft at the destination on a fine day with hours of fuel in reserve, the decision may not have to be so time critical, such that the diversion ultimately takes place from overhead the destination. Whatever the time frame may be, once the decision is made, get the plan into action without further delay.

Creating a Diversion.

When it becomes apparent that the flight is about to differ from the original plan you may choose to buy some time as you get your cockpit in order and your mind around the decision making process. There's already a time saving if you've been smart and reviewed what is available at each of those circled airports as you've flown past and possibly even made some notes. Notwithstanding there is still much to consider, so throttling back to a lower power setting will both save fuel and offer some reprieve in terms of time, particularly if you've already flown passed your best option. If the weather is less than ideal, extending a stage of flap may be a wise consideration too, offering a lower stall speed and greater forward visibility. Just remember to reconfigure to the appropriate cruise configuration once you've commenced the diversion.

When the decision is made, start with an approximation of the new track, the distance and time interval. This can be refined once you are pointing in the right direction, but the priority must initially lie with setting a new course. In the first instance, circle where you are and note the time, circle where you are going and draw a line between the two points. Estimate the new track and measure off a distance using your ruler, or a suitably marked pencil. Using your aircraft's 'nil wind' speed, work out a time interval and factor in a few minutes if you're astute enough to appreciate that there will be a headwind or tailwind. Do you have enough fuel to fly the new interval and arrive with reserves intact? If the answer is "no", then you'll need to seek out a nearer option. If the answer is "yes", then let's start diverting the aeroplane without further ado.

Once established on the new heading. Aviate, navigate and then offer a little communication. Advise flight service of your flight plan amendment and your new destination and ETA. This is just a brief, initial transmission as there is still work to be done; however, it is also important to let people know if you have diverged from your flight plan so that they know where to start looking in the case of some further drama. Once they are advised, it is back to the business of refining your diversion.

There are numerous things to consider once you're on your way, but the first efforts must be directed to verifying your initial planning and refining the details thereof. Established in stable flight, check the alignment of your 'Directional Indicator' against the magnetic compass and verify that the heading you are flying is reasonable to take you to your new destination. Observe the planned track and see if any ground features on the chart correspond to any features outside the window as this may give an early indication of wind effect and the resulting drift. While on that topic, revisit the forecast wind, or better still, the wind you encountered prior to the diversion. Draw an arrow from that direction on your chart to assist in orientation and then calculate the drift.

With a new heading calculated, confirm the distance to run and re-calculate the ETA at the next waypoint and ultimately your destination. Make a mark at the mid-point of the sector for a gross error check of calculations. Now, just fly the aeroplane for a while and take a breath. Manage your fuel and navigate for a period and firmly establish your new track in your mind, for it is at about this time that the initial angst of the decision-making process will start to subside.

With a clear head you can attend to the detail. Review the significant terrain in the area, the proximity of airspace and restricted areas and verify the latest weather and NOTAMs for your new route and destination. Write down the critical details and frequencies for your destination and tune any relevant navaids and GPS equipment as required and available. Always work 'up' from the basics, that is to say that the manual planning should come first and then the electronic wizardry brought into support the procedure. The manual calculations will give you a far more detailed appreciation of the task and terrain, whereas technology alone can lead you astray quite quickly. Between the two, safety is greatly enhanced.

When the diversion is completed and the tasks have all been attended to, make a simple review of what has just transpired. Evaluate the different stages of the process to ensure that the boxes have all been ticked. When you're confident that the matter is well in hand, sit back and aviate as normal.

Keeping Focus.

With a well planned diversion underway and the hard work done, there can be a tendency to let the mind wander. In the wake of all the excitement, it would be real disappointment to run a fuel tank dry or make some other fundamental error. Fall back on basic procedures. Always, Aviate-Navigate-Communicate. You may now be headed for an unfamiliar airfield with different procedural requirements, so prepare as well as possible without eroding your primary task of managing the aeroplane.

Avoid sweating about issues that you can't control, or that can wait. Things such as the 'welcoming committee' awaiting your arrival at the previously planned destination, or the fuel agent's phone number at your new one. These things can wait. When you are on the ground, parked and safe, the 'administrative' issues can be attended to. Worrying about them prematurely can only negatively influence your original decision or subsequently erode your performance in the cockpit.

On arrival at your revised port of call, a whole new set of decisions will rear their head. Do you now continue onto your original destination? Is the weather now suitable and is there enough daylight? If I stay the night, when will I depart tomorrow? Your mind will be racing, but you won't get hurt unless you get back in the aeroplane prematurely. Take your time and 'if in doubt-bug out'. A diversion of this nature occurred for me on a charity flight around Australia. My family and media were waiting to greet me at my destination, but as I stood on the ground at a fuel stop and scanned the skies I could not be assured of a safe outcome. Was I disappointed? Yes. But with many hours of experience in my logbook, I still decided that discretion was the better part of valour and tied the aircraft down for the night. A decision vindicated that evening as the rain pelted down on my hotel roof.

Safety First.

At some stage along the way, all aviators are confronted with the possibility of diverting. Safety must always be the overriding principle with the absolute power of veto. Pre-flight planning can assist greatly when called to make the decision to divert, but regardless of the degree of preparation, make the decision like a pilot in command. Gather the information, review the information, analyse the options, decide and evaluate the outcome. Most importantly, decide and act in an informed, measured manner.

A managed diversion is really a fairly straightforward exercise, albeit with a potentially high workload. It becomes challenging when the decision to divert is left too late, or if the decision is to continue in the face of overwhelming evidence to the contrary. This is when a pilot can become boxed in and run out of options. Deciding early, managing the situation and playing it safe are the keys to a successful outcome. So when the flight ahead starts to raise more questions than answers, it may well be the time to start planning a diversion.

Points to Remember.

* In aviation, as in life, things do not always go to plan.

* Often the most difficult part of the diversion is the initial decision to go elsewhere.

* When the diversion is safely underway, review the decision and subsequent actions to confirm that nothing has been overlooked.

* Safety must always be the overriding principle.

CHAPTER SEVEN

FLYING THE APPROACH TO LAND

What goes up, must come down and for every successful flight, its end is marked with an equally successful return to earth. Only occupying a fraction of the flight time, the landing continues to provide a focal point for pilots, passengers and the chap on the hill with the telephoto lens. Why is it when the wheels meet Mother Earth, sometimes it's a kiss and sometimes a slap? Often the answer lies well before the flare.

Method or Mystique?

Many words have been written and hours of briefings undertaken in search of mastering the ability to majestically land an aeroplane. Some have been scientific and even mathematical in nature, while others have been far more general. For pilots, part of the problem is that landing is a mixture of both science and art. It involves not only the hard figures of approach speeds, aircraft weight, environmental conditions, flap setting, and available runway length, but the judgement of when the appropriate control inputs need to be initiated and then modulated to guide the aircraft back to earth. Blend into the mix the varying ambient conditions of wind and temperature and the pilot is challenged by an act of complex co-ordination.

As such, the input of a flight instructor and the age-old art of 'practice makes perfect' are often the best means of managing the individual's manipulative issues. However, there are a number of fundamental matters that each pilot can attend to that will make the instructor's lot much easier and go a long way towards improving the approach and landing phase.

Often very unfairly, a flight is judged or remembered by the landing. The preflight planning, standard operating procedures and navigational finesse that brought the aircraft safely over the runway threshold are too often overlooked when the flight terminates with a less than gracious arrival. My own mother expressed a degree of dissatisfaction with my landing in a Boeing 737 one very wet and windy night at a very challenging airfield. Needless to say we had a polite chat, and a laugh, later. However, this culture can serve to exacerbate the pressure to perform that some pilots feel and ultimately climbs into their concentration, eroding their performance even further. This is human nature, yet if we look at automation; it doesn't suffer from such subtleties.

Advanced modern aircraft equipped with sensors and coupled autopilots routinely conduct 'Autolands' as the pilots watch on in the role of an interested monitor. These emotionless autopilots resist the tendency to over-control and are without trepidation as the ground looms large ahead. It is purely an exercise in calculation and function, timed precisely for a successful outcome. Even so, automation on aircraft may still have defined limitations such as crosswind, beyond which the pilot must intervene. As such, the need still remains for the pilot to be the manipulative master of the aeroplane and yet regardless of experience, the landing phase can turn and bite. Some of the reasons are those faced by student pilots every day.

The Goal.

It is firstly worthwhile to review what is sought from landing an aircraft. The smooth 'greaser' should not be the ultimate goal, though it can be a rather satisfying side-effect. In fact, on wet runways, the aircraft manufacturers recommend a firm or positive touchdown as an extra defence against aquaplaning.

Safe landings are about arriving at the aim point, on the centre-line at the required airspeed and aligned with the runway. As long as the touchdown is not unduly heavy, bounced or askew, the goal has been achieved. The degree of comfort will be enhanced with a lower rate of descent at touchdown, but this should not be the driving force. Undue focus on the smooth touchdown can lead to the consumption of significant amounts of valuable runway as the pilot 'feels' for the ground. And even after such an effort, if contact hasn't been made by the time the airspeed has eroded below flying speed, the aircraft will thump onto the ground anyway. Wasted runway, wasted effort.

Safety must always come first. Finesse will come with experience and maintained with currency. When the goal of the landing is clear in the mind, it serves to reinforce and clarify what is being sought on final approach; aim point, speed and centre-line.

Relax.

Before the manipulation skills even come into play, the mind has to be on the job. For any phase of flight, the pilot must be well rested as fatigue will erode the performance and safe conduct of any flight. As the landing by its very nature comes at the end of a sector, fatigue may be at its very worst, so rest should always form a critical element of pre-flight preparation. Yet beyond the physical fatigue, pilots can induce a degree of mental fatigue by focusing too much upon the landing well before it is even an issue. This can serve to distract the pilot from the tasks at hand and eat at the holistic viewpoint that is needed for sound flight management. It is best to preserve the mental energy until it is actually needed.

Tell-tale signs can also start to creep in and instructors over the years have seen them on numerous occasions. Often nervousness manifests as the landing pilot starts to discuss the prevailing weather conditions in a negative sense as if to offer an excuse for the upcoming performance. There is no argument that hot, gusty conditions, or low visibility present their own challenges to the landing, but idle banter doesn't help. Review the conditions and consider how they may best be countered before the aircraft is flying down the final approach. Do the gusts warrant a speed additive on final? Where is the crosswind coming from and what actions are required to be aligned with the runway at touchdown? May a higher flap setting lower the nose for better visibility in passing showers? Respond to the conditions with an assessment and a plan rather than nervous tension and a negative chatter.

White knuckles are another sign that the landing holds some demons for the pilot. Strangling the control column does not threaten the aircraft into flying better and actually destroys much of the pilots 'feel'. It can lead to subconscious control inputs and poor trimming of the aeroplane. Both of these actions can interfere significantly with the flaring process where there exist major changes in pitch and power.

Similarly, a pilot's posture can interfere with the landing. Whether through fatigue or stress, pilots can often slump or lean to one side as they fly the final approach. This can play havoc as landing is about appreciating the perspective of the runway ahead and a constant 'picture' is one of the best aids. At the flight's commencement the seat was adjusted in an unrushed manner based on the best outlook, so any slumping or leaning is going to adjust that set of visual cues. I know personally at the end of a long day and late at night, I have to consciously remind myself to sit up straight to retain the frame of reference ahead that I know.

Often these traits are subconscious and build gradually beneath the surface as the landing draws closer. In the training phases, there is an instructor there to offer a wake-up call, but once licensed, pilots must take this task upon themselves. Whether flying an Instrument Landing System (ILS) or sliding down a visual approach, use a cue to prompt a self-review. It may be the selection of the final stage of flap, a certain height or capturing the glideslope, but at some point take a moment to remind oneself to sit up straight and relax. Take a breath, adjust the posture and relax the grip on the control column to feel if the aircraft is *really* in trim. You are now physically ready to land the aeroplane.

Be Consistent.

It always pays to have a consistent set of terms of reference. The environment and the aircraft can introduce enough variables, so it is important that we endeavour to keep our methods constant.

As mentioned, one of the first items we can attend to for landing occurs even before engine start; seat position. Logically, seat position determines our 'eye position' which is critical in the process of perspective and judgement. Some aircraft provide a series of markings or guides for the best eye position, though the majority leave the seat position up to the individual. Internally, the seat must be far enough forward to comfortably access all controls and switches while permitting full and free movement of the control column at its aftmost travel. For those aircraft with fixed seats and adjustable pedals, the same effect can be achieved through the use of cushions. The position should also permit a clear view of all instruments and annunciators without being obscured by the instrument panel coaming. (This can sometimes be a challenge with ageing, drooping coamings and another reason they need to be maintained.)

For the view outside, the positioning of the seat should permit a clear view ahead above the instrument panel. Commonly, pilots can sit a little low, but ideally they should have a view along a tangent down the nose. This will ensure an adequate forward field of vision in low visibility operations. This seat position is best assessed on the ground just before engine start. To do it any earlier may result in having to repeat the process after you move the seat to access a jacket on the back seat, or close a door.

Scan the instrument panel, exercise the controls fully and look well ahead to visualise the landing perspective. The perspective will be different on approach, but the selection of flap will lower the nose further and enhance the outlook. If flying the same aircraft day after day, this exercise may come naturally, but take a little more time and effort when moving between aircraft. On approach with the seat adjusted correctly, remember to sit up straight and the eye position will offer a relatively consistent perspective on each approach. It is worth noting that if the seat position doesn't feel quite correct coming in to land; LEAVE IT ALONE! Do not adjust seats on approach as the potential catastrophe from a seat sliding back is not worth the attempt.

It is often said that a good landing results from a good approach. This is fundamentally because a good approach involves being configured in a timely fashion, with correct speeds being flown and achieving a stable rate of descent. It may be flown from a base leg or a straight in approach, so the perspective can change. What remains consistent is that the approach is unrushed and the pilot is able to focus on the approach and landing without being distracted by gross adjustments of airspeed and/or attitude late in the approach. Should these occur, the safest option is generally to go-around and attempt another approach to land.

If new to a particular aircraft type, not overly current, or even just a little uncomfortable; establish the aircraft into its landing configuration of gear and flap setting early in the approach. It will result in slowing down early and powering up against the extended drag, but it allows the aircraft and the pilot to be established in the landing 'mode' without being rushed. With the landing checklist complete, there are no other tasks to distract from the primary one of flying the approach. There should be no further major changes in attitude or trim and the 'picture' out the front should remain fairly consistent down to the flare.

Once stable and configured with landing gear and flaps on final approach, the aim point should be clearly selected. If not marked by a painted stripe, it may be abeam a group of trees or a darker patch of dirt. Whichever it is, the pilot should pick the spot and keep it steady in the windscreen by whichever technique they have been instructed. However, the eyes should not be obsessed with the aim point. There must be scanning cycle that assesses the approach perspective, or 'slope', the track relative to the centreline and even a brief glance back inside to verify the airspeed. A mental repeating mantra of something like; 'aim point-slope- centreline-speed' may remind the pilot to continually assess the various aspects of the approach.

Importantly, if something is not correct, fix it before moving onto the next point, always being aware that adjusting one element may impact upon others. As the approach gets closer to the ground, the adjustments should become progressively more subtle, notwithstanding that 'windshear' and the like call for significant action regardless of the aircraft's location.

Correctly flown, a stable approach flown with a consistent, cyclic scan will bring the aircraft over the fence in a healthy state to commence the flare. A 'last look' inside may be stolen to indicate whether the speed is a little fast or slow or trending, but otherwise the eyes are outside. The subsequent transition to the flare calls for the pilot to look ahead and release the rigid eye-line from the aim point.

Ground Rush.

The runway is now just below the wheels and the flare is about to commence. Much of the hard work has actually already been completed, so what can go wrong now? How can a stable approach be complicated at the last moment, or in some cases much earlier? There are a number of variables in play from over-controlling to cross-winds. When the wheels approach the earth some of the challenges are of the pilot's making and others are most definitely not. This is when the fun begins.

Points to Remember.

* Safe landings are about arriving at the aim point, on the centre-line at the required airspeed and aligned with the runway.

* Being nervous and 'strangling' the control column does not threaten the aircraft into flying better and actually destroys much of the pilots 'feel'.

* * If the seat position doesn't feel quite correct coming in to land;

LEAVE IT ALONE!

CHAPTER EIGHT

LANDING YOUR AIRCRAFT

As we saw in the previous chapter, a good landing is often intrinsically linked to a good approach. An unrushed stable approach, flown in a consistent manner delivers the aircraft across the threshold in a positive state, ready to return to the earth. Even so, things can go awry. However, the good news is that the problem often lies with some sneaky repeat offenders that can be readily put in their place.

Was it *really* that bad?

Ultimately, a poor landing is merely the symptom of a root cause. Identify the problem and it can be fixed; no drama. So let's not allow the dread of a bad landing crawl into our finite mind space and further erode our confidence and subsequent performance. Firstly, review why the landing was 'bad' in your opinion. If it was in the ball park of aim-point, airspeed, approach profile and runway alignment, then it's quite possible it wasn't really a bad landing. Perhaps the arrival was not subtle, BUT IT WAS SAFE!

If there were symptoms such as a bounce, a prolonged float or directional control issues on touchdown then we assess them for what they are and address the contributing factor or factors. Either way, there is no place or need for self-punishment or depression. If you drop the football, pick it up, move on and try a bit harder next time; you haven't lost the game. Flying will always present challenges and in part, that is the fun. Very few are endowed with a mastery of any art, it is better in this business to be honest and consistent because that equates to safety. So let's look at some of the culprits that endeavour to sneak under our guard as the wheels move to meet the runway.

On the Numbers.

At the optimum speed, the aircraft is endeavouring to arrive with a safe margin over the stall speed while touching down at a speed that is slow enough to minimise the ground roll and wear on the undercarriage and airframe. Two of the most common complaints relate to long landings and hard landings. Often both can be traced back to the same issue of airspeed. Long landings can result from carrying excessive airspeed into the flare, whereas a hard landing can result when speed is on the low side.

Long landings can absorb copious amounts of runway very quickly. As an aircraft floats down the runway, the chance of an overrun is increased, while extra stress on the undercarriage and brakes often result as they are wrongly used to compensate for the wasted runway in the flare. Airspeed above that recommended, or calculated for a given weight, equates to additional energy. The additional airflow over the wing results in the aerofoil continuing to provide lift when the task at hand is to land the aircraft. This resistance to landing can be further exacerbated by the thicker air immediate to the surface known as 'ground effect'. Furthermore, a higher airspeed results in more control responsiveness and that subtle flare manoeuvre now results in the aircraft flying away from the runway.

At the other end of the spectrum, should we lose too much speed and energy in the flare, the aircraft will decide when it is going to land and gravity will play a far greater role than inertia. With low airspeed the controls can feel less responsive and the control column can seemingly be at its aft limit with nothing to left to offer. There is no flaring left to be done and the aircraft will simply arrive firmly on the runway, unless we have fortunately timed these events with such precision that they occur just as the wheels touch. Generally though, the aircraft will fall from its flare height to the surface with a thud, if not a bounce.

So speed is premium to maintain control effectiveness into the flare and achieve the anticipated responses from our inputs and achieve the desired landing performance. Again, a stable approach is one of the best means to the correct airspeed on entering the flare. Configure the aircraft to land and get used to the attitude and feel nice and early. Turbulent conditions and hot days will present a challenge as the airspeed needle flickers, but aim to keep a constant attitude out the front. As the runway looms near, most pilots sneak a 'last look' at the airspeed; just a glance, nothing more. Accordingly, the airspeed can be noted as high or low resulting in a slightly earlier reduction in thrust, or perhaps the need to carry it later into the flare to prevent the energy washing off totally.

And don't underestimate that sixth sense in the flare. If it feels like your backside is falling out from under you, trust your instinct and increase the power to arrest the sink. Energy and speed are critical elements in landing, yet long and hard landings are not solely the fault of inadequate speed control. That would be too easy!

Hit the Spot.

As we fly down our final approach we are always assessing our aim point. That imaginary spot on the runway where we project our flight path will lead us to connect with the runway. A stable approach sees that aim point sitting steadily upon the same point in our windscreen as we drive towards it at the nominated approach speed. Unfortunately, that spot can sometimes wander up and down the windscreen.

'Nailing' that aim point is more commonly referred to as aim point retention. A frequent scenario sees the aim point move further down the runway in the latter stages of the approach. Sometimes this is because in the heat of battle the pilot loses a degree of discipline in focussing on the specific point, lost in the looming runway. Occasionally, it results from trepidation on the part of the pilot manifesting in unwarranted back pressure on the control column, raising the nose. For some larger types it can stem from the increased effectiveness of the elevator as it enters ground effect. In any case, the touchdown point will occur much further down the runway, just as if excessive speed had been carried into the flare.

Equally, 'target fascination' with the aim point can result in the pilot arriving at the correct point, but driving it into that point rather than flaring. In the worst case the nosewheel can actually touchdown first, causing damage or a potential 'wheel-barrowing' situation; neither are advisable. This issue can be particularly significant at night as the landing lights illuminating the runway almost transfix the pilot's line of sight to the tarmac at the very point that the eyes should start to look ahead. The goal is to retain the aim point until we arrive at that wonderfully vague point in space where flight down to the runway transforms into the landing manoeuvre known as the flare. Hold onto the aim point for too long and the aircraft will most certainly make an arrival rather than a landing.

Just as with speed control, aim point retention or lack thereof, can be a contributing factor in the 'where' and 'how' of an aircraft's landing. Often aim points can wander or become hypnotic when pilots are tired at the end of a long day, or a session of circuits. Be aware of where you are looking and work at flying there, but also be ready to release the point when the flare dictates.

Showing Some Flare.

The flare is undoubtedly one place where aviation science and art frequently speak a different language. Even for the most experienced pilot, the judgement call of when to transition into the landing manoeuvre can be misjudged. It is a skill that only comes with practice and a rite of passage that all students must endure along their journey. However, just as precision in parking a car improves with time and familiarity, the visual cues will begin to establish themselves in the pilot's mind's eye with greater exposure.

At that point when the approach becomes the landing, the pilot's eyes should release the aim point and rise towards the runway's end. This is sometimes easier said than done, particularly at night when the sight of the landing light's beam on the runway can prove almost hypnotic. Still, it is at this point that the ground will rise in the peripheral vision and assist in judging the rate of closure while the focal point ahead will offer cues for maintaining directional control. The pilot is now endeavouring to bleed the energy from the aircraft by reducing power and increasing the angle of attack with back pressure. Lift is still being generated, but without adequate energy, level flight is replaced by a controlled descent toward the runway. Occasionally, the reduction in power is not complete and the aircraft may elect to continue flying in ground effect, so make sure that when it is time to land, the thrust is reduced fully.

Playing it Straight.

The need to be aligned with the runway at touchdown has been previously emphasised. It avoids directional control issues during the ground roll and undue trauma to the undercarriage. The most obvious challenge to this objective is the crosswind and instructors and students continue to battle this fiend using a variety of techniques from the 'side-slip' to the 'crabbed' approach where the aircraft is aligned in the flare.

Yet at times, the wind does not need to be abeam for runway alignment to wander. On final, pilots can develop a 'wing walk' where they oscillate aileron, or occasionally rudder, inputs with a resultant rolling or yawing motion. Presenting as gentle S-Turns as the pilot chases the centreline, it is often merely a case of P-I-O; (Pilot Induced Oscillation). PIO can occur with the use of elevator as well and results in a lot of effort for no benefit. If centreline management is proving a struggle on final, then relax all control inputs and see if the aircraft is actually trimmed and flying well. The problem may simply be over-controlling, which if carried into the flare can cause all sorts of confusion.

A Thought on Short.

A short field landing is achieved by flying a standard approach at a slightly lower speed and achieving the desired touchdown point with precision. It is NOT achieved by a very low speed/high thrust undershoot approach, dropped onto the near end of the runway and followed by excessive braking. This latter technique has more holes in it than Swiss cheese as it doesn't account for obstacles on approach, avail adequate thrust and airspeed to conduct a missed approach and runs a high risk of flat-spotting a tyre. And yet you will see it time and again.

Short field landings are more than ever about a stable approach, flown at a minimum safe margin speed over the stall. The standard approach perspective means that no major adjustments in technique are called for and those trees on final are not a threat. Aim point retention is doubly important as these approaches are generally necessitated by length critical airstrips. At a lower speed, there will be less energy to dissipate, so the landing flare is initiated a fraction later. This assists in achieving the aim point and avoiding an unwanted float down the runway. Fly the book figures as they appear in the Flight Manual and always verify the field length is adequate from the 'performance charts'. And check that adequate length exists to depart again before committing to a landing is always well advised.

Airmanship and Away!

In all landings, AVIATE-NAVIGATE-COMMUNICATE. In a tight traffic environment, don't succumb to subtle pressure from ATC to expedite clearance of the runway. As an aviator, airmanship dictates that you won't dawdle unnecessarily on the runway after landing. Jumping on the brakes and blowing a tyre or snapping a nose-gear won't help anybody. You are the pilot in command, fly the aircraft to the best of your ability and if inadequate separation has been provided with the following aircraft then they can go-around. Similarly, these requests can be made over the radio as the aircraft is rolling out and should not be acknowledged unless the aircraft is well and truly decelerated and under control.

In all cases, on approach, in the flare, or after a bounce, if the pilot is not happy with the situation then conduct a missed approach. As the saying goes, "If in doubt. BUG OUT!" Generally, the earlier a poor situation is abandoned, the simpler the extraction. Time affords a more organised abandonment of the approach in an unrushed manner. For this reason, the go-around should be practiced at various stages of the approach and landing throughout a pilot's career. It is a manoeuvre that can be called for at any time and requires the correct sequence of actions and the management of trim that can prove awkward. A prudent, competent missed approach is a strong weapon in a pilot's arsenal.

For all of the variables that the aircraft and environment can provide, it will always be impossible to detail them all in the written word. Similarly, nothing can substitute the positive input from a proficient instructor for both the student pilot and the qualified aviator who is lacking currency. What this chapter has sought to emphasise is the common traps that plague the landing phase and to emphasise that the landing is not the 'make or break' of a pilot.

The landing is merely the arrival at the end of a flight that has called for all manner of skills enroute. Highly rated and unfairly judged, the landing will continue to be the secret nemesis of many pilots. However, in its most basic components it is about being on speed, on aim point, on slope and aligned with the runway. When the ground rush is sensed and the earth moves up to meet the wheels, it is all about safety........subtlety will come with time.

Points to Remember.

* Do not allow the dread of a bad landing crawl into our finite mind space and further erode our confidence and subsequent performance.

* Airspeed is often the root cause of both long landings and hard landings.

* A short field landing is NOT achieved by a very low speed/high thrust undershoot approach.

*At any stage, on approach, in the flare, or after a bounce, if the pilot is not happy with the situation for any reason then conduct a missed approach. If in doubt, BUG OUT!

CHAPTER NINE

THE TRUE MEANING OF PILOT-IN-COMMAND

Very few people ever forget the first time that an aircraft was taken aloft and returned safely to earth solely under the guidance of their own hand. That first solo flight signifies a variety of matters from piloting to personality. For many, it is also the first time they experience a real sense of command.

Who's the Boss?

In the melee that is modern society it is very easy to be lost in the crowd and become just another number. Motorists essentially need to display a style of command when they drive their vehicles, yet it is obvious that many either fall short or blatantly disregard the responsibility. We may find leadership positions in the workplace or on the school sporting fields, but it is also entirely possible to remain concealed in the masses. There is no such place to hide in the cockpit as a licensed pilot.

As the first solo flight becomes imminent, the sense of command begins to surface in the psyche. For some it is relished and others it is met with a degree of self-doubt, but for all it is an essential quality in an aircraft pilot. It is the realisation that there is no fall back and that every decision and act of manipulation is assessed an enacted by the pilot in command. It was once rather zealously phrased as, "You fly alone. You die alone." Whilst dramatic in the extreme, it underlines the solitary nature of that first flight and therein lays both the trepidation and the absolute satisfaction.

It is the satisfaction of commanding an aircraft in flight safely. After that first solo, the feeling is nothing short of euphoric and rightfully so. Yet the euphoria will naturally dissipate as a level of familiarity is spawned with experience, although that appreciation of command should not. From that first solo, rather than sitting meekly as a front seat passenger, a new mindset should be born that consistently asks, "What would I do?" This mindset should remain for the rest of your flying days; alone or with passengers, privately or commercially, whichever road you decide to travel.

Command means that the responsibility rests with you from pre-flight until the aircraft is tucked away in the hangar. It is about thorough preparation and care for passengers, situational awareness and airmanship, decision-making and so much more. Even so, it should not be perceived as a burden, merely the way in which you approach your flying. Once instilled, the qualities that enhance command can also flow on in a positive manner to other aspects of life.

In Good Company.

A pilot possesses a duty of care for those on board the aircraft. Passengers, whether they be fare-paying folk or friends, will need positive direction when it comes time to take flight. This direction may start well in advance of the engine starting.

Firstly, look the part; it's easy. There is no need to dress like a Vice-Admiral, but swim shorts and loafers don't really portray a professional image either. Clean sensible attire and attention to personal appearance for the flight will make a far better impression upon your passengers.

The airport environment beyond the glass is alien to most people and they may not understand or perceive potential dangers at hand. Be it refuelling facilities or spooling down turbo-props, each has their own associated threats. Setting the example with a positive pace along marked walkways, or guiding your passengers where these do not exist is essential. Passengers may well wish to stop and take photographs, so supervise this carefully as backing away blindly to get an aircraft in frame can have lethal consequences at an airfield.

Aircraft can be very awkward to board and passengers will often require assistance. Always ensure that the focus on one passenger boarding or another's photography does not allow the others to roam aimlessly. Highlight a safe area with bounds where they can wait while you attend the matter at hand; often this area may be the 'triangle' from wingtip to tailplane. Once on board it is critical that emergency briefings are not a machine-like formality. Highlight the exits and harnesses and where possible, have the passenger unfasten and re-fasten their belt to your satisfaction. They will remember this in the heat of an emergency far more readily than a verbal brief.

Front seat passengers need special attention as they have vital flight controls within easy reach and possibly their own exit through which to evacuate in an emergency. Advise them that they can look, but don't touch with the exception of items like air vents. Once again, run through as many points by action as possible, or by read-back at the very least. It may be worth breaking it down into non-aviation, bite size pieces. For instances, exiting a Piper Cherokee in an emergency from the front seat may call for the passenger to unlock the overhead latch, the door handle and their seat belt. Tell them it's as simple as 1-2-3 and have them run through it and call the numbers, 1-2-3. If you are incapacitated they will be the key for the passengers in the rear row to exit as well. Also, ensure that the front seat passenger's seat is FIRMLY fixed in place prior to flight. A panicked passenger sliding back on take-off will grab onto anything and the control column is dead ahead; not what you want on rotation!

With all passenger management, communication is the key. The information and instructions should be relayed in a positive, professional manner. Often a simplified explanation assists in the process and can go a long way to easing apprehension. Let them know that you don't anticipate anything going awry, but this is the best time to make them familiar with the aeroplane. This brief will not only serve the interests of safety, but instil the passengers' confidence in you as a pilot.

Master or Manager?

In operating an aircraft, the pilot in command needs to be both master and manager. It calls for the co-ordination of numerous tasks beyond the pure manipulation of the aircraft that call for management skills. Additionally, operational decisions will need to be made and at this time the role of master must surface; but even the master should still use managerial skills to effect the decision. This is commonly known as Crew Resource Management, or CRM.

Pre-flight considerations involving fuel and weight and balance or the fundamental 'go or no-go' decision will often test the mettle of the pilot in command. With a base line of the regulations, company policy and personal safety, buffers will be applied to these decisions. At times the most difficult decision will involve disappointing passengers, be it a cancelled flight due to a serviceability issue, weather or any one of a range of reasons. Disappointment is offset to a high degree by pre-fixing all explanations with the phrase, "in the interest of safety." There are very few rational people that will argue that line of thinking.

Still this doesn't make breaking the news any easier, but it is the difficult moments that test command's true substance. There may be external pressures, be they commercial or a personal desire to get home. Yet the decision must be made based on fact and the best information available. This is the case whether it is a local scenic flight or crossing the Pacific and whether cancelling pre-flight or having to divert in flight. Going with the flow and taking the soft option is easy, but in aviation can have disastrous outcomes for those who choose to do so. Persevering into less than ideal weather when supposedly VFR is one such instance and how many pilots have died wishing they'd turned back?

Standing your ground takes a degree of inner strength and may often involve more work to find a solution; however, command isn't about shirking effort or responsibility. Leadership is better than that and is never more tested when things go wrong.

Emergency.

When, despite all of your careful preparation, it does still goes wrong the pilot in command must step up and take the challenge head-on. That doesn't mean that you rush in to meet the challenge, but you definitely stand your ground and consider the options carefully. It can be a fine balance between a measured response and drifting into procrastination when there is a pressing emergency.

Rushing in is fraught with danger, but loitering when a fire is threatening to burn through the main spar of the wing is equally injudicious. Personality will play a part in the individual's response just as it will in the ability to take command at any time. However, study and thorough preparation does more than simply instil knowledge; it instils confidence and this is a vital trait when the chips are down. Combined with self-discipline, these are two critical weapons in a pilot's arsenal to defeat the onset of confusion and panic.

In an emergency, the pilot may be the only one who fully understands the severity of the moment. Passengers may over-estimate or under-estimate the significance of the emergency, but regardless of their perception they will look to the pilot to provide leadership and remain in control. Time permitting; they will also be seeking reassurance.

A pilot's responses at all times need to be calm and measured. Emergencies will dump adrenalin and surge the heart rate, but the solution lies in positive rather than panicked behaviour. We are all human and susceptible to pressure to varying degrees, however, when in command of an aircraft cool, calm leadership is the order of the day; the panic can set in once you're back safely in your own bed.

A State of Mind.

Command is not about gold bars on sleeves, nor is it defined by the size or role of an aircraft. Command is a frame of mind that really begins its journey after that first flight. It is more than the acceptance of responsibility; it is a genuine understanding and preparedness to be proactive.

Confidence, leadership, ability, knowledge, management and airmanship are all facets of the concept of command. There is no single, magic factor that defines command. Nor is there a point that one knows it all; this is the point where confidence becomes usurped by its ugly cousin, complacency. To lead effectively, you never cease to learn or listen and the arrogance of complacency will very quickly stifle both of these necessities.

From first solo to flight deck, pilots must recognise that to fly effectively they must command effectively. They must command their aircraft, their passengers, their crew and themselves. And none of these entities appreciate being spoken down to or mishandled. An effective commander will lead, manage and even empathise with apparent ease. Ultimately, it will be their manner and professionalism, not their wings or epaulettes that commands respect.

Points to Remember.

* Command means that the responsibility rests with you from pre-flight until the aircraft is tucked away in the hangar.

* Passengers are the pilot's responsibility and they may not be familiar with the ways of aviation and the potential dangers.

* Command is not about gold bars on sleeves, nor is it defined by the size or role of an aircraft. Command is a frame of mind that really begins its journey after that first flight.

CHAPTER TEN

THE PILOT'S COMFORT ZONE

The rules of visual flight are well stipulated and are designed to keep the non-instrument rated pilot out of harm's way. However, the craft of successful visual flight is more than merely measuring visibility or distance from cloud. It is about the ongoing assessment and application of a number of personal parameters that are more restrictive than the regulations.

Am I Legal?

Safety in aviation should always be the foremost goal. Whether it is a quick scenic flight with friends or a trans-continental long haul flight with hundreds of fare paying passengers, the primary obligation of the pilot is to ensure the safety of all on board. It is not an exercise in ego, or an absolute promise to arrive at the destination on schedule or even that day; it is about the duty of care for all on board and those whose roof tops we overfly.

Through harsh lessons of the past and the ongoing review by

governing authorities, guidelines and regulations have been established to point us in the right direction. However, there has never been a rule book, manual or computer program that is able to cover every scenario or cater to the varying levels of ability of the masses destined to apply the information. By their very nature, regulations tend towards the conservative side and rightly so; that is the safe thing to do. Yet even then the regulations may not be conservative enough for some individuals or difficult to apply in the real world.

Visual Flight Rules (VFR) are classic instance where the interpretation and application of a defined standard can prove difficult. They involve fixed parameters, calibrated in units of distance for inflight visibility and the separation from cloud. Fixed units which are measured in the potentially highly dynamic air mass through which we fly. Cloud bases fluctuate and visibility can shrink in the blink of an eye. This can be challenging stuff!

Furthermore, the average ability to gauge height and distance is, at best, marginal. One only has to look at the wide variation of responses from aircraft asked to report at 3 miles when there is no GPS or DME to assist them. To take this judgement and apply it to the fluid world of weather raises the bar to a whole new level. Even so, as part of our cycle of activity, pilots must continually endeavour to assess the prevailing conditions against the legal requirements, bearing in mind that these are absolute minimums. Below these we are illegal; however, we were probably approaching an 'uncomfortable' situation some time before we actually reached the minimum requirements.

To safely operate in the visual flight regime, there is a need to not only strictly adhere to these pre-defined constraints, but tailor them to our own individual standards and the conditions that are set before us on the day. And all such tailoring MUST be applied on the CONSERVATIVE side of the equation as the countryside is marked with the wreckage of those who thought that their personal standards were better than the regulations.

Am I comfortable?

Flying should be enjoyable. Even when it is a paid profession, there should be a degree of gratification every time the world falls away from the wheels. That's why we do it. There is very little fun to be had getting boxed into a corner which may ultimately cost your life. As such, one of the first and foremost questions a pilot should ask is, "Am I comfortable with this situation?"

This question can be applied to many aspects of aviation, but in the visual flight sense it rings particularly true as an early warning system. Generally speaking, well before the visibility drops to the minimum required or the fin starts cutting the nimbostratus, the heart rate will elevate and the hair on the back of the neck will start to twitch. This should serve as a signal to the pilot that they are starting to get towards the deep end of the pool; their feet may still be touching the bottom, but for how long?

The 'comfort threshold' will vary from person to person and change as the individual gains experience, hence the difficulty in applying a broad standard as defined by the regulations. The crosswind limit on an aeroplane may be 20 knots, but lack of crosswind currency may render an inexperienced pilot to hesitate at going flying in those conditions. It would be legal, but would it be prudent? A dual check with an instructor would be a safer option and a sensible application of personal standards. In-flight weather is just the same. 5 kilometres visibility or 500 feet vertical separation from cloud may be legal, but may not be 'comfortable' to everyone.

In flight, at the first sign of discomfort with any particular scenario, the pilot should look at removing themselves from the situation or at the very least, critically review their circumstance and options. All VFR flight should be conducted with a 'back door', or a means of escape. It is foolhardy to continue towards deteriorating weather conditions but absolutely fraught with danger if the weather behind is also going bad.

Am I Orientated?

An escape route should be ever-present. At all times the VFR pilot should have a ready-made answer for, "Where would I go if...?" When the rain is thrashing the windscreen or visual reference is silently lost in cloud, it is often too late. Furthermore, the stress and workload of the situation will not permit the brain to offer the best resolution. Flailing charts and turning knobs will rate a poor second to keeping the aircraft upright and out of harm's way.

Continually through a VFR flight, the pilot should be aware of the nearest landing field and ensure that there is a clear route to it. It may be a private airfield or a farmer's crop-duster strip, but it is an option and should not be released from clear access until another presents itself ahead. The field does not have to be in sight, but access to it must be apparent. Even with 5km visibility, if there is no clear route to a landing field it means that the pilot will be forced to possibly conduct a precautionary landing on an unprepared surface should the weather close in further.

To have suitable options and an escape route, it is vital that the pilot remains orientated and 'situationally aware'. 'Situational awareness' can be defined as *"...being aware of what is happening around you to understand how information, events, and your own actions will impact your goals and objectives, both now and in the near future".* To be aware of what is happening around you and how that may evolve requires the pilot to continually review the situation.

BEFORE the weather even approaches the minimum legal levels for VFR flight, the pilot should have a clear picture of where they are and where they are going. This should include an awareness of the location and elevation of the highest terrain in the area and possibly setting a 'personal' minimum altitude based on that information. Remember that sneaking up a valley in poor visibility can also be a trap as power-lines may be draped between the ridge lines. Additionally, the high surrounding terrain may nullify the path of a pre-determined escape route and even prevent a safe 180 degree turn.

As well as an awareness of potential landing fields, utilise all available navaids to support your visual navigation and refine your exact position. They will provide critical distance and bearing information to assist what you see on your map. GPS is a tremendous tool in this instance, but can also come with the pitfalls of over-reliance and complacency for the visual pilot.

Outside of the three dimensions of flight, a critical element of situational awareness is that of fuel and endurance. Fuel equates to time, distance and options. If we have the fuel, we may hold clear until the shower passes at the field, navigate around the offending weather or divert to another airport or possibly our point of departure. When the weather is approaching our 'personal minimums', fuel management can be overlooked as aviating and navigating consume a greater part of our finite brain-space. Running a fuel tank dry, or worse, total fuel exhaustion is the last thing we want to occur at this time.

Being orientated and situationally aware at all times is critical to the ongoing assessment required for visual flight. It is best appreciated continually when the weather is in our favour to allow earlier and safer in-flight decisions. Leaving anything to the last minute in aviation has never been a good idea.

Am I Safe?

We have considered the legal minimums, reviewed our options, assessed our personal comfort level and appreciated our orientation. If we are not satisfied with any aspect of this exercise, we are pushing our limits and had better look at rectifying the situation. This is always best achieved sooner rather than later,

It is quite possible that the pressure is already beginning to mount by this stage and the age-old adage of AVIATE-NAVIGATE-COMMUNICATE should be remembered; fly the aeroplane! At this time, inadvertent entry into cloud, a loss of altitude or an unusual attitude could be catastrophic. A level 180 degree turn out of there may well be the safest option.

Visibility is critical. Rain and showers will reduce it below the minimum in a flash. Flying with minimum separation from the cloud base also often results in poor visibility, so if the terrain permits, afford some more clearance from the cloud and its scrappy under-hang in an effort to see further ahead. But beware of lowering cloud and rising terrain leading to the classic trap for the unwary pilot.

Pre-flight cockpit organisation and a sound ongoing cycle of activity may prove to be one of your best friends. Reaching over to search for and tune up multiple frequencies and leaning down to look for a chart are sources of distraction from the primary task of flying the aeroplane. You should already be orientated and if you need one chart, it should be easily accessible and brought up to eye level to read. 'Head down' operations should be avoided at all costs. This is another reason why fuel management is important. Ideally you don't want to be reaching down to change tanks at this time if it can be avoided.

Aviate-Navigate-Communicate. Fly the aeroplane first and maintain control. Assess terrain clearance and extricate the aircraft to a route clear of weather. It is better to divert early, rather than leaving it too late. As we have said before, "If in doubt, BUG OUT!"

Similarly, there is often resistance by pilots to ask for help, yet the sooner they are able to advise air traffic services, the possibility exists of their assistance in the form of radar vectors clear of terrain where the service is available. When out of the immediate harm's way, double-check the management of fuel before the engine goes quiet and ensure that enough fuel is available to execute your new plan. Of course, the flight would have been best served if these plans were in place from the outset and an early decision had prevented flight in deteriorating VMC.

In the Zone.

VFR flight is a genuine skill. As such, it needs to practised and honed just like any other skill. It is not easy, but that is one of the challenges of flying and a source of satisfaction.

Sound preparation and efficient management of the cockpit will aid greatly in offsetting the potential chaos. A sound ongoing cycle of activity will make sure that the house is in order the day when the weather foe comes knocking. Four questions at the heart of that cycle are;

Am I legal?

Am I comfortable?

Am I orientated?

Am I safe?

When the situation is deteriorating, these answers are not as straightforward and this is a sure-fire signal that action is needed. Execute any plan sooner rather than later and always Aviate-Navigate-Communicate.

By looking beyond the regulations and applying personal buffers, a greater margin of safety results. These 'buffers' do not need to be numerical in nature, they may simply be the fact that the evolving situation makes the pilot uncomfortable. By exercising prudent judgement and always placing safety at a premium, a greater level of enjoyment can be forthcoming from the tremendous endeavour of flight. And all the while remaining in our comfort zone.

Points to Remember.

* Safety in aviation should always be the foremost goal.

* Am I legal? Am I comfortable? Am I orientated? Am I safe?

* Safety can involve an ongoing assessment and application of a number of personal parameters that are more restrictive than the regulations.

CHAPTER ELEVEN

A Forced Landing.
Lessons Learned

I am one of the fortunate pilots to have had an engine failure in a single-engined aircraft and walk away unscathed. In the wake of that forced landing, I gained an even deeper insight into a manoeuvre that I had be practising and teaching for a good many years.

In this chapter we will look at some of the lessons that I learned from that close call, but first here is the story of how it all unfolded…

As an Approved Test Officer (ATO), I enjoyed the task of testing candidates for the issue of a shiny new licence or rating. By and large, the students were well prepared, knowledgeable and very keen. On a June afternoon in 1993 I was tasked with a Commercial pre-licence test for an overseas candidate who was champing at the bit to return home and join his national carrier. Clear skies, an aeroplane fresh from its 100 hourly maintenance inspection and a diligent student set the tone for a pleasurable flight; well, for the first couple of hours anyway…………

THE PRACTICAL PILOT

Azlan possessed a very quiet manner that somewhat belied the fierce determination with which he approached his flying training. As he leaned over the wing of the Aerospatiale TB20 Trinidad and re-calculated his endurance and performance figures, he was a picture of concentration. To this point we had successfully navigated our way to a distant port of call. He had flown the aeroplane smoothly and countered the periodic 'examiner-induced challenges' that inherently crop up during a test flight. From here it was on to another country town, thence a return to Sydney and hopefully a recommendation for the fully fledged licence test. His preparation and planning had been superb and his chosen routing reflected his comprehension of my perennial pre-cursor; "bearing in mind that this is a single-engined aeroplane". A philosophy highlighting that a few extra track miles over topographically friendly territory can present a pilot with fields and features that can assist in navigation and provide options should things go quiet up front.

With the paperwork completed and more than adequate fuel evenly distributed between the two wing tanks, we fired up and launched once more into the beautiful skies over this rural region. Once established in the cruise, I adopted the role of employer and advised Azlan that the 'passengers' at our next port had cancelled their flight and he was now to return to Sydney, "bearing in mind that this is a single-engined aeroplane". With a line feature in the form of a highway a short way ahead and the security of a navigational beacon and an airstrip, a little planning would result in a fairly straightforward trip back. In the only tarnished point of the flight, Azlan guesstimated a heading and wheeled the aircraft eastward to point in the general direction of Sydney. The proposed route was relatively void of features and characterised by the mountainous 'tiger country' of the Great Dividing Range. Whilst seemingly a poor option, he was not breaking any rule and was acting 'In Command

Under Supervision' (ICUS). At worst it was questionable technique and a de-briefing point, after all that is what training is all about.

As we skirted to the south of a small township, Azlan came up for air, refined his heading and made good a direct track to Sydney. Whilst clipping along at 1,500 feet above ground level (AGL), I felt a little uneasy, though not unduly so. Despite rumours to the contrary, single engine aircraft do not immediately enter 'auto-rough' at night, over rugged terrain or on Trans-Pacific ferry flights. Whilst not perhaps prudent, our track was perfectly legitimate.

I was midway convincing myself of this fact when a flickering of light caught my eye. The Trinidad's digital fuel flow gauge was hopping around without rhyme or reason, whilst the engine continued to purr and the good old fashioned analogue fuel flow needle sat like the Rock of Gibraltar. New-fangled gadgetry, maybe, but either way it prompted me to look outside for a potential forced landing field; just in case. As luck would have it, a lone small clearing was just off the right and I asked Azlan to enter a gentle turn toward it. He had still not noticed the 'Digi-Flow' jumping around when I drew it to his attention and started to talk him through the trouble-shooting process. When the analogue needle started to reflect the readings of its digital counterpart my interest heightened and we completed an FMOST checks without delay. The engine now began to surge in company with the cockpit indications so at this point I took over and called up Sydney Flight Service to put them in the loop. I had gone from 'fat, dumb and happy' to 'rather concerned' in the grand total of about ninety seconds.

Our lone paddock approached beneath and the surges were becoming so significant that the maintenance of height was becoming an increasingly difficult task. I advised Flight Service that we were 55 miles from Sydney on the 255 radial whilst I still had the chance as *radio contact had been 'in and out' at this height. I was contemplating a precautionary landing with the remaining sporadic power when total engine failure took me out of the decision making process. I trimmed for the glide and knowing that radio communication was at a premium, alerted Sydney of our worsening predicament and manually switched on the Emergency Locator Transmitter (ELT). Again through the checks; no luck. Fortunately, I had already decided upon the field and a course of action, though it was becoming increasingly apparent that it was going to be very tight and far from a smooth ride. I briefed Azlan and told him that when we were on the ground, he was to exit and get clear of the aircraft without delay.*

Assured of making the field, I started configuring the gear and flaps and advised Flight Service that I would shortly be going 'no-comms' as I switched the electrics off in an attempt to minimise the chance of post-impact fire. The world was getting very big in the window and as I aligned myself with the field I decided that it was way too short to make it over the trees on the approach and still pull up by the far end. As I had done at airstrips in the outback and New Guinea, I slipped the aircraft down between the trees in an effort to maximise the effective length. The foliage rushed by, there was a short squeak of the stall warning horn and then the wheels hit. Thump!

70 knots or so across an unprepared surface is a wild ride. I was on the brakes, keeping straight and hoping for the best when a sizeable rock jutted up ahead. Unable to swerve to any great degree, I braced thinking this was going to hurt. I tensed my guts and for a nanosecond thought of the control column spearing into me. Bang! The right gear struck the rock and we were OK; hurtling across the paddock, but OK. With not enough room for my liking, I heaved back on the stick and kicked in right boot, effectively 'ground looping' a nosewheel aeroplane. The right gear seemed to give at this point and we slewed sideward, shuddering to a halt short of the trees. I swung around to tell Azlan to get out. With the disturbed dust still suspended in the late afternoon air I was looking at an empty seat, an open gull wing door and the northbound end of a southbound student. He sure knew how to follow instructions!

I joined my breathless candidate and having taken a moment, returned to a rather forlorn aeroplane. Paranoia forced me to inspect the Trinidad's tanks which revealed adequate fuel both sides: Phew! I tried calling up on radio and thankfully established contact with an approaching Cessna 310 who had already been diverted to the area. I advised the pilot that we were all OK and he relayed to Flight Service our exact position and further information. (He had one of those new-fangled GPS things.) It was getting dark and with the temperature dropping, we threw on our jackets and gathered kindling in case we were here for the night. Fortunately, the rescue helicopter was on the job and making a bee-line through the night sky to our position. Once in range, I described the field, potential hazards and where the aircraft lay in the paddock. (In my previous life as a paramedic, establishing a landing field had been part of the training.) Without further delay I heard the thumping rotors and spotted the chopper's lights to which I replied with every light, strobe and beacon the Trinidad possessed. The helicopter's spotlight turned night into day as he manoeuvred with due caution and touched down a short distance away. I returned the aircraft to a dark, lifeless state and we were guided by the crewman to the waiting helicopter. Strapped in, the rotors spun up and we rose into the absolute darkness, steadily accelerating into the void. Slowly the glow of Sydney's lights became a visible horizon and I knew we were on our way. It was at this point that I think I stopped to draw a breath. I was headed home.

Many years have passed since that winter afternoon, but the lessons gleaned from the experience are still with me. Firstly, my philosophy of track selection in single-engined aircraft was upgraded from a preference to a personal doctrine. Whilst recognising that it is not *always* possible, the trade-off of extra track miles must be made when friendly terrain is on offer. Always be aware of terrain, lowest safe altitudes (LSALT), nearby airfields and navigation beacons in the planning phase when you are on the ground, unpressured and with the time available. Even when venturing into instrument flying and multi-engine aeroplanes, icing conditions and single-engine ceilings call for a healthy respect of the LSALT and surrounding topography.

Since my first flight, I have always had one eye out the window for a potential forced landing field when I've been flying single-engined aeroplanes. For the thousands of hours looking, it probably only made a real difference for me on this one occasion, but it was literally a lifetime full of difference. Being aware of my only option, deciding to turn towards it and formulating a potential plan *before* things deteriorated fully probably saved my neck. It is important to utilise the available time to its full potential as it is measured in seconds when it's running out and equates to the rapid loss of valuable altitude. My actions weren't the hallmark of exceptional skill; they were simply the application of the training we all receive as licensed pilots.

Another reason that we walked away that day was that I was current on practice forced landings (PFLs) and as a former bush pilot, I had a fair amount of experience on short airstrips that were void of asphalt and touch-down markers. My currency at the time was due to my job as a flight instructor, but ever since that day I have insisted on a dual check in my private flying to ensure that I'm still up to speed on unexpected occurrences such as engine failures and go-arounds.

In addition, bush flying gave me an appreciation of speed control and the feel of an aeroplane at the slower end of the performance envelope. It gave me a greater sense and appreciation of the symptoms of low speed flight and the approaching stall than is necessarily offered by the warning devices fitted to aircraft. Flying the aircraft at slow speed cruise from time to time can also serve as a worthwhile reminder as to how an aircraft 'feels' with less relative airflow and slipstream passing over the control surfaces.

Also, you don't need to be flying out of rough, short and sloping runways to practice short-field flying. Even if your flying is always out of long, sealed airstrips it is good form to integrate some short field arrivals and departures into your comings and goings. Challenge yourself to fly accurately and really endeavor to achieve the touchdown point. You never know when you may need to call upon these skills in anger.

When any emergency occurs, the briefing to your passengers must be concise as time will be of a premium and in their panic they will probably only be able to process a limited amount. Brief the key points of any emergency actions prior to flight, such as harnesses, doors and anything else of importance. Have them actuate the doors and demonstrate the securing and release of a seat belt. Reassure them that while you don't anticipate an emergency, it is always best to be prepared in advance. Your professional approach to safety will instill them with additional confidence in your ability as a pilot.

A great way to assist with currency of any flight manoeuvre is 'armchair flying'. Whether it is practicing a forced landing or preparing for an airline simulator check, there is great value in sitting in a chair and rehearsing the procedures. And don't hold back, speak out aloud what you would say to passengers or on the radio and move your hands and head as if you are flying the aircraft. The more practiced the procedure, the more 'brain space' you will have available to make decisions and process the variables that will undoubtedly occur on the fateful day.

THE PRACTICAL PILOT

When you touch down on an unprepared paddock, the world slides past very quickly. Every rock, ridge and tree stump appears to be racing towards you and your steering authority is not nearly as responsive to the grip of rubber on asphalt. That rough landing roll and subsequent deceleration is far from subtle. Fortunately, with two pilots on board, I was able to ask the other pilot to ensure that all loose items were secure prior to touchdown. When flying solo or with non-aviator friends, this might not always be an easy task. As you load your aircraft, consider where equipment is stowed, giving due consideration to the fact that they may become a projectile in certain circumstances.

Post impact, consider any remaining switching to minimise the risk of fire that you have not already completed in the air. Exit the aircraft when it comes to a halt and check on the welfare of all on board, attending to those in need of first aid as a priority. On this point, a first aid kit is a valued piece of equipment on board any aircraft and should be checked before flight. Similarly, I was forced to land on a mountain range in the middle of winter. Even though the cockpit had a heater, I always carried a jacket and cap within arm's reach and not just in case of an emergency landing; heaters fail too.

As with all aspects of flight, the overwhelming priority is to fly the aeroplane. I used to be an 'air judge' for spot landing competitions and on occasions would see participants lower their heads seeking bonus points for verbalizing their checks as the aircraft spiraled towards the ground. AVIATE-NAVIGATE-COMMUNICATE has always been a mantra of aviation for a very good reason. Be aware of the best glide speed for your aircraft and trim for it. Endeavour to complete all of your checks, but continually monitor the aircraft's state and the progress of your descent towards the field. Airspeed maintenance is critical as your best glide speed for your weight will offer the best gliding range, bearing in mind the effect of wind.

THE PRACTICAL PILOT

Equally important, one never wants to allow the airspeed to deteriorate and lead to a stall and loss of control.

Personally, I lost a degree of innocence that afternoon. I had always looked upon *every* patch of urban clearing as a potential forced landing field, which in retrospect was more than a little naïve and over-confident. I am now a little more selective. Funnily enough, my first flight back after the forced landing was a couple of days later in the form of a candidate's single-engine night cross country test; talk about getting back in the saddle! I can now confess to very sweaty palms a couple of times that night. Notwithstanding, I have continued to fly and enjoy single engine aeroplanes ever since. The experience has in no way deterred me from 'singles', it merely reinforced my belief in how they should be operated.

Statistically, engine failures are not a common occurrence. That does not relieve us as pilots of the obligation to be prepared for the loss of engine power. It is an obligation to ourselves, our passengers and those who dwell beneath the sky we transit. As in all aspects of aviation, sound knowledge and preparation can give a pilot a distinct advantage. The advantage can in turn be pressed home, with the maintenance of skills and a common sense approach to all aspects of the operation. Aviation is about setting and meeting our own standards, not merely those imposed by instructors, examiners and test pro-formas.

Points to Remember.

*When possible, plan a flight with due consideration to the terrain being transited and the options available.

* Always be aware of the forced landing field options that are

THE PRACTICAL PILOT

available at any given time.

* Practise short field landings and glide approaches when possible

* In any emergency, maintaining control of the aircraft remains the top priority. AVIATE-NAVIGATE-COMMUNICATE.

CHAPTER TWELVE

THE GO-AROUND

In any undertaking, persevering with an undesirable situation is ill-advised and aviation is no different. As in life, sometimes those situations are of our own making, sometimes through the actions of others and sometimes we are just in the wrong place at the wrong time. The reason why becomes irrelevant as our focus should really lie in extricating ourselves from our predicament. The 'go-around', or 'missed approach', is one means for pilots to do this when approaching to land.

For the purpose of this chapter we shall use the term 'go-around' as it is most commonly used in flight schools. Often the term missed approach is associated with instrument flying, so here, we'll discuss the go-around.

A Critical Phase.

The approach and landing is a critical phase of flight. The aircraft is descending towards the ground, most likely changing its attitude, power settings and configuration and most likely in close proximity to other aircraft. To the backdrop of radio transmissions and checklists, the pilot is called upon to exercise judgement and manipulative skill within a narrow corridor of operation. It's a challenge – and that's why we like it so much.

However, by its very nature, the approach and landing is subject to numerous variables. Air traffic control requirements, environmental fluctuations, aircraft limitations for extending flaps and landing gear and the presence of other aircraft. In all honesty, there are too many to list. I have discontinued an approach because another aircraft entered the runway and I have discontinued and approach because twenty kangaroos entered a runway. I have been on the final approach to land when I have spotted fence posts across a runway, placed there as part of a land dispute between neighbours. And I have 'gone around' simply because I was not happy with how I had flown my approach to land. Consequently, long before a go-around is even an issue, it should be considered as a real possibility in the planning stages of a flight to ensure that adequate fuel is always available to go-around.

Unless a more pressing issue such as a major structural failure, fire or lack of fuel dictates that you must land immediately, the old adage of "if in doubt – bug out!" is well advised. The go-around allows breathing space, while taking the aircraft away from the ground. The pilot can re-examine the reason for going around, make a decision and organise the subsequent course of action in an unrushed manner.

Manoeuvre or State of Mind?

The very first component of conducting a go-around is making the decision to do so. At times this is simple and on other occasions it is more challenging. If the runway is occupied by another aircraft and there is nowhere to land, a go-around is the only option. However, if the wind is fluctuating about the crosswind limit of the aircraft, the choice may seem to be more difficult. Taken a step further, if the approach is being flown a little above the ideal airspeed, a little above the ideal approach path and you don't want to appear to have made a mistake in front of the passengers who are also personal friends. In this case, personal pride and ego can start to encroach upon sound decision making if we let them.

An early decision is generally a conservative and good decision in aviation. That being said, how do we define 'early'? In a general sense it may be that first point when you feel uncomfortable with the approach. You may be having trouble slowing the aircraft down to extend the landing gear or recognise that you are higher than you should be at that point in the approach. For whichever reason, not only is the aircraft beginning to fly away from the desired profile, your escalating concerns are insidiously eroding your situational awareness and your ability to fly the aircraft. Tunnel vision on one aspect of the approach will undoubtedly be at the expense of the others. The point at which this uneasy feeling arises will change with experience, but regardless of hours in the log book, if there is cause for concern, there is a case to go-around.

Airlines will often define a 'stable approach' that must be achieved by a certain height or a go-around MUST be initiated. The parameters of that stable approach will include limiting tolerances on such items as speed, flight path, rate-of-descent and the completion of checklists. We could well apply such a philosophy to our approaches in light aircraft too, considering centreline, slope, speed and checklists. In fact, 'centreline – slope – speed' is a common cyclical scan employed by some pilots on approach.

Perhaps 500 feet above the airfield would be a suitable point to nominate that if the approach is not stable at that point, then a go-around should be initiated. However, let's not forget that an early decision is a good decision, so if the aircraft is too high and too fast on the downwind leg, then discontinue the approach and reposition for another attempt.

Unfortunately, too often it is the reluctance to abandon an approach that can lead to poor outcomes. In the case of so many landing accidents, the pilot's first lament is that they should have gone around rather than pressing on from a poor position. In this way, the go-around can at times be as much a state of mind as a manoeuvre.

Considerations in Flying the Go-Around.

The technique for flying a go-around will depend on the particular aircraft type and even the point that a go-around is initiated. Early in the approach, the aircraft may merely be levelled off and flown back for a second attempt, whereas a go-around in the flare introduces a great many variables. At the core of the go-around is to increase power to full and fly the aircraft safely away from the ground at the nominated airspeed for the manoeuvre, retracting the landing gear and flap as specified for the type.

Once the decision to go-around has been made, the aircraft is effectively transitioning from an approach to land to climbing away as it would after take-off, however, it is not quite the same. A planned take-off roll begins with the aircraft trimmed correctly and with the appropriate flap setting for the aircraft to smoothly transition into flight.

The first component is to increase power to full. On some types, this may call for the mixture to be set to 'rich', the propeller pitch to 'fine' and 'carburettor heat' to be set to 'cold' to ensure full power is achieved. Know what is required for your particular aircraft.

And while the power should be set promptly and smoothly, throttles should never be slammed forward to the firewall. This is the time that you want the engine to be your friend, so don't slap it. Without an accelerator pump, some engines will struggle with harsh throttle movement while more advanced turbo-charged engines may 'over-boost'. Know your aeroplane, its systems and limitations and then treat them with care and respect.

When full power is applied for the go-around, the nose will have the tendency to pitch up and combined with an aft trim setting presents an undesirable situation. If allowed to develop, the nose will not only rise, but the airspeed will erode and this is dangerous. On increasing the power, positive control of the aircraft's attitude is vital. Remember that the pilot always flies the aircraft and not the other way around.

In the case of a go-around it is highly likely that the aircraft will have a greater amount of flap extended and a more aft trim setting than for take-off. The landing flap setting is designed to permit a steeper approach path, a lower approach speed and greater forward visibility. However, when the go-around is initiated, fully extended flaps provide a great deal of drag and can hinder the subsequent climb. Consequently, the flap will need to be raised at some point to allow the aircraft to obtain the desired climb performance. That being said, the flap should be raised in stages, allowing the airspeed and performance to increase and stabilise before the next stage is raised.

There may also be a yawing moment associated with the increasing power, just as there is on take-off. Once again, positive control inputs will be required to prevent the yaw and to maintain the aircraft in balance.

Many manuals teach the technique of POWER – ATTITUDE –TRIM to go-around. Refer to the manual for the particular aircraft and always refer to the flight instructor, but the key point here is that after increasing power, ATTITUDE comes before TRIM. Physically fly the required attitude and when the situation is stable use the trim to subsequently relieve the control forces. Failure to do so may result in an undesirable high nose attitude and an even less desirable erosion of airspeed.

A less aerodynamic reason for the nose pitching up can be a pilot's tendency to pull back in a low level go-around because the ground is very close. Don't be phased by this as an aircraft can go-around even after touching down and is one way of dealing with a bounced landing. Attitude and airspeed are what keep the aircraft flying, regardless of altitude.

With full flap extended, the initial climb performance may be poor and a level segment may need to be flown to accelerate the aircraft to a safe speed for flap retraction. Don't be phased by this, be patient and methodical.

Once the aircraft is safely climbing away and 'in trim' can some other variables be considered. Is there an aircraft taking off below, perhaps it would be wise to climb out slightly to one side of the runway? Bearing in mind this may not always be possible at airfields with parallel runways. If operating at an airfield with a control tower you may need to advise them that you are going around and listen for subsequent instructions to re-join the circuit.

However, always AVIATE – NAVIGATE – COMMUNICATE in that order. Ensure that the aircraft is flying with sufficient airspeed and then fly it to a safe place in terms of altitude and tracking. With this under control you are then in a position to communicate.

Be Prepared.

At all levels of aviation, the go-around is an under-rehearsed and frequently poorly executed manoeuvre. Yet it is the most likely abnormal situation we are to encounter when compared to an engine failure or something similarly rare. As discussed, the reasons for a go-around can be many, initiated by ourselves or made necessary by external circumstances. Consequently, we should always be prepared to go around, mentally and manipulatively.

Armchair flying is the cheapest way to practise. Sitting quietly in a room and flying the manoeuvre in the mind's eye, moving the hands and feet as if increasing power, combating the pitch and yaw and configuring the aircraft. Even better, fly the manoeuvre in the cockpit of the actual aircraft on the ground when the engine isn't running, touching the various controls just as you would when flying. A cautionary note, ensure that the aircraft isn't powered and you don't inadvertently flatten the battery, or worse, retract the landing gear!

As an instructor and test officer, I included a go-around in every dual check. At every opportunity, I would have the student fly a go-around and it was consistently a challenging manoeuvre. I have seen it mishandled by private pilots and airline pilots alike and the core reason is not a lack of ability, it is a lack of practise. Always be prepared for a go-around.

If in Doubt.

Flying an aircraft is a challenging skill requiring discipline, judgement and co-ordination among other qualities. Flown in the dynamic environment of the atmosphere and subject to so many variables, it is no wonder that sometimes the best laid plans go awry.

THE PRACTICAL PILOT

When an approach and landing is not progressing along the lines of the safe standard that you seek, or even if you just don't feel comfortable - rather than indicating poor flying as some may perceive, a go-around reflects sound judgement and positive command by the pilot. These are qualities that indicate sound airmanship whereas as manipulative skills are a function of repetition. Airmanship and command judgement are qualities that are far more difficult to teach and learn. If in doubt… bug out.

Points to Remember.

* A go-around is as much about possessing the correct mindset as it is manipulation of the aircraft.

* You can go-around at any time and generally, the earlier – the better.

* Always practise and be prepared for a go-around on every flight.

* Remember there may be significant changes in pitch and trim during a go-around.

* Power – Attitude – and then Trim.

* A go-around demonstrates positive command judgement. If in doubt…bug out.

CHAPTER THIRTEEN

DECISIONS, DECISIONS

They say that our life is the sum of all of our decisions. Like some sort of organic flow chart that forks with 'yes, no and maybe' to lead us down a new and unknown path. At times, flying can almost fall into the same category, with an equal number of frustrating choices and loathsome grey areas. Recently, another aircraft was lost, caught up in the midst of descending weather and rising terrain. On hearing the news, I went through the frustrating round-about of 'if only' and wondered at what point there was no way out and at what point the pilot realised this.

Life's choices are also similar to aeronautical decisions in that our own experience can be a major factor. As an adolescent, we all tend to be a little more impetuous and impatient, with no real experience to use as a slide rule by which to gauge our actions. At that age there is very little ability to project forward and see how this might play out, we are far more 'in the moment'. At the controls of an aeroplane, an inexperienced pilot can be similarly affected. Without a sound appreciation of their own boundaries and little exposure to the proven limitations of those that have gone before, our decisions may lack the 'fear factor' of an older hand. That healthy feeling of hair standing up on the back of the neck that says. "I've been here before" or "I've read about this". These mental checks are often the first 'red flag' that the present situation is starting to erode and a decision is needed.

An Acquired Skill.

The ability to make a decision can be an acquired skill of the mind, just as landing and aircraft is a skill of the eyes, hands and feet. As a flight instructor, I have always been aware that teaching the manipulative skills of flying is the relatively easy part. Instilling airmanship, discipline and prudence is far more difficult. That involves influencing the perspective and behaviour of another, and that is never an easy task. Older students sometimes struggled with the 'pushing and pulling' of the aeroplane, but with life experience they generally grasped the mind-set easily. Younger students, even those with great skills, sometimes found that possibly dying as a consequence of their actions to be an abstract concept. However, age and experience could not be seen solely as the defining factors either.

Experience can invite a new threat, as the demon 'complacency' can creep into the mind of the most capable aviators. Some years ago, a good friend of mine perished attempting a low-level manoeuvre with insufficient altitude or energy. He was a good pilot and a great guy, but his comfort zone had undoubtedly encroached upon his common sense on this occasion. A decision made on an impulse, on the spur of the moment, can have ramifications that last a lifetime for so many people.

Furthermore, there are legal decisions and prudent decisions. The rules and regulations may lay out the required visibility or maximum crosswind, but these are legal limits. Our own level of experience, currency and personal 'comfort zone' may determine that we choose an alternative option before the legal limits are reached.

Making a Decision.

There are numerous 'models' to be found on the internet that lay out a formal method to make a decision. It may sound strange to have a formal process for a mental activity such as decision-making, but like many actions in an aircraft, a checklist can be of tremendous benefit when we are under pressure. Such a process can save valuable time when the overwhelmed mind is tending towards procrastinating and wondering where to begin. Still, it is best to find a model that suits you.

One example is the **F – A – T – E** process. It stands for;

Fly the aircraft.

Analyse the problem.

Take Action.

Evaluate.

FATE is a very simple model but it importantly begins with flying the aircraft. In-flight events and pressing weather can distract us from the primary task of flying the aircraft if we allow it to happen. Next we analyse what our actual problem is and then take action. It is always important to evaluate our decision at the end of the process to ensure that the required outcome meets our needs and that we have actually attended to the problem. For instance, the decision to divert to another airport due to weather may be a sound move, but in subsequently evaluating the decision we may discover that we have overlooked the amount of fuel required to fly there. Evaluating our decision offers a chance to take a breath and calmly reassess.

Another time to evaluate any decision is at the flight's completion.

With the safety of the ground underfoot and no pressures bearing down, it can be a time to reflect whether you would handle the situation differently next time. This personal debrief after a flight is invaluable in extracting the maximum value out of any experience and building up a mental library of situations to assist with similar events in the future.

The Funnel.

An early decision is often a conservative decision. It may be take place even before take-off when serviceability of the aircraft, fading daylight or a poor weather forecast is cause for concern. Airborne, when deteriorating weather or shrinking fuel stocks start to become a factor, it is probably time to act. For the moment that concern enters the brain, it sucks up the very mental processing capacity that is needed to make sound decisions. This capacity is finite and seemingly shrinks as pressure increases.

Developing situations can be viewed as a funnel. At the beginning there is a wide mouth where time and options are plentiful. However, the further you fly down the funnel, your options become less, be it deteriorating weather or diminishing fuel reserves. Additionally, as the funnel narrows, the narrower your focus may become as the pressure builds, eroding your broader, overall situational awareness. Turning back, diverting, even out-landing in a paddock may be inconvenient, but YOU are still in control. Once you put the external forces in the pilot's seat, you are entering very dangerous territory.

Equally dangerous is the temptation to make no decision at all and blindly continue down the funnel, hoping things get better. Firstly, that niggling voice inside that things are developing badly takes up valuable brain capacity, eroding concentration. Ultimately, if the situation deteriorates, a decision will be forced on the pilot and unfortunately the funnel may be very thin by this stage with no room left to manoeuvre or options available.

I have always believed that aviation is not inherently dangerous, but it can be incredibly unforgiving. For those that have danced with the devil and survived, the spectre of a hill in the clouds or a coughing engine has changed their outlook for the better for the rest of their days. However, their survival was more often through good luck than good judgement. It is a risky business to learn by taking the situation to the very edge of the envelope and that is best left to the trained hands of test pilots. We mere mortals are far better advised to play the safe hand and extricate ourselves before our apprehension becomes desperation. Take the early turn, the easy road and contemplate what may have been from the safety of an airfield.

Decisions, Decisions.

Aviation is a skilled act undertaken in an unfamiliar environment. We are the guests of the Gods when we leave the earth. There are so many variables that may influence our journey along the way; the compressed time-frame of travelling at speed, the whimsical nature of the weather, the challenges of our own skill level, complacency and a need to get home. Like turning screws, their pressure grows with every minute that passes and every drop of fuel consumed. All the while, our mind is taxed and our human frailty is exposed.

It is a joy to fly in the skies above, but it is a privilege that is bound by our own human limitations. Our decisions mark the points at which we answer those challenges set before us and unfortunately those decisions can literally be a matter of life and death. Opt for an early decision, on the conservative side of the fence and live to fly another day. For those very decisions may lead to long-lasting outcomes for you and the ones you love. Fly safe my friends.

Points to Remember.

* An early decision is generally a safe conservative decision.

* Making a decision is a skill that can be learned, practised and improved, just like any other.

* Experience can aid decision-making, but always be wary of complacency.

* Have a process to aid in making a decision. F-A-T-E is just one example.

* Developing situations can be viewed as a funnel. Act early when options are available.

CHAPTER FOURTEEN

Fuel for Thought.
PRE-FLIGHT

Fuel is at the very heart of each and every powered flight. From the planning phase to the execution and the post flight review, fuel is a key component of safety, efficiency and commercial profitability. However, this precious liquid has also been a major player in a high percentage of the accidents and incidents since Orville and Wilbur first took to the skies.

Fill 'er Up?

In recent times, aviation fuel has been receiving its share of media attention for its impact on the environment and how airlines and manufacturers can best offset these ramifications. As bio-fuels are researched as a future means of powering aircraft, airlines are paying microscopic attention to their fuel carriage and subsequent consumption. Fuel equates to weight; therefore, you burn fuel just to carry fuel; it's a vicious cycle.

Amongst this commercial scrutiny and the search for more fuel efficient flight lies a more fundamental issue for the aviators amongst us. At its most base level, fuel offers the pilot two valuable commodities; time and options. Yet simply carrying more fuel does not offer all the answers as the management of fuel covers a broad spectrum of issues. The individual aircraft's fuel system, legal requirements, pre-flight planning, aircraft performance and in-flight management are just a handful of the considerations where fuel comes into the frame.

In general aviation aircraft particularly, the balance of fuel and payload is an ongoing juggle with very few types offering full seats AND full fuel tanks. A compromise is often the best available solution and this can only be safely reached after due thought and ongoing review. Fuel management is a dynamic aspect of flight that calls for sound judgement from the first flight plan to the final shutdown.

Know Your Thirst.

The fuel systems of very similar aircraft can be vastly different. It is critical to thoroughly understand a particular aircraft's fuel system well before the endorsement flight ever takes place. From single tank 'on/off' operations to multi-tank pressurised systems with scavenge pumps; each aeroplane has its own way of feeding fuel to the engine. Even the most advanced systems can be compromised by ambiguous placards, switches and unreliable gauges, so the onus is upon the pilot to understand exactly how the system operates. Failure to understand this process can leave the engine literally gasping for air, sometimes even with fuel on board.

The fuel selector is the core component of the pilot's interface with the fuel system and may be as simple as merely selecting fuel 'on' or 'off'. Yet even the most basic systems have suffered from the incorrect selection of fuel. This can result from reasons as diverse as poor ergonomics to misleading signage, which can be further compounded by a poorly lit cockpit. Just some fuel selector traps over the years have been the passage through 'OFF' when changing tanks from left to right, placards at 90 degrees to the actual plane of movement of the selector and training aircraft with the fuel selector virtually beyond the instructor's grasp. All of these issues have been managed safely over time, but it is important to have a heightened level of awareness of the pitfalls. For all types, clearly understand the various selections, detents and direction of movement of your fuel selector.

Unfortunately, in many light aircraft, these less than ideal fuel selectors can be supported by less than ideal gauges. From inaccurate readings to fluctuating needles, gauges are there to support the calculations and visual inspections which define how much fuel is on board. Fuel quantity must always be verified by more than one means, and it always pays to be very wary of the cockpit indications.

The fuel system can also be made up of a series of tanks beyond merely 'left' and 'right'. Mains, auxiliaries, nacelle and belly tanks are just some of the configurations existing in a complex fuel system. In turn, fuel can on occasions be transferred between tanks or 'cross-fed' to an opposing engine. It is vital that the capacities of this array of tanks, the sequence of their use and the effect on the Centre of Gravity be thoroughly understood. Failure to do so has seen all manner of problems in the past. From burning the Centre of Gravity out of the operational envelope, resulting in controllability issues to inadvertently venting fuel over-board, the ramifications of not understanding a fuel system are both broad and potentially catastrophic.

Selectors, gauges, boost pumps and tanks all make up an aircraft's fuel system and each can offer their own pitfalls. A thorough endorsement, handling notes and flight manual can all go a long way to educating pilots on the idiosyncrasies of a particular type. It is also worthwhile speaking to pilots who have operated the type extensively as they can frequently offer an insight into some of the traps of the type, often borne of personal experience. Safe fuel management begins with a sound knowledge of the fuel system.

Plan, Plan, Plan.

The safest seat on an aeroplane is the chair in pre-flight briefing. It is not moving at 3 miles per minute, nor is it directly affected by enroute icing conditions or engine failures. However, it does offer a relatively stress-free opportunity to consider such misadventures.

Fuel planning has become a science from which numerous computer programs have evolved, offering savings of millions of dollars to global airlines. Breaking this science down, fuel planning fundamentally seeks to provide enough fuel to operate the aircraft over the desired sector with a margin of safety, meet the regulatory requirements and cater for reasonably fathomable eventualities. The first two points are functions of calculation and regulation, while the latter calls for the less tangible skill of judgement which is enhanced with the accumulation of experience.

Calculating the fuel required on any particular flight is a basic skill of flight training. After making due allowance for the climb segment, the wind is considered to derive a ground speed and then the time interval is factored by a known fuel consumption rate. Basic navigation meets basic mathematics, and yet it can still go wrong. It was a relatively simple case of confusion between kilograms and pounds that led to a Boeing 767 ultimately becoming a glider due to fuel starvation. The potential for this still exists as there are aircraft with quantity gauges in US gallons and fuel flow in pounds per hour, even though avgas is purchased by the litre and weight and balance is calculated in kilograms. It is a veritable minefield at the planning stage and can have an even greater impact at the end of a long day. A gross error check of your expectations against your figures is healthy in all aspects of aviation, but particularly in fuel management. Additionally, always double check the 'Fuel Plan' section of any flight plan for obvious arithmetic errors and anomalies.

Regulatory requirements then seek to round the 'flight fuel' upwards with allowances for various contingencies. 'Variable Reserve' seeks to allow for any number of......well, variables. Inaccuracies in forecast ground speed, differences in actual fuel consumption against those planned, additional manoeuvring in the approach phase and so on. 'Fixed Reserve' is the absolute minimum that should be in the tanks when you are reunited with Mother Earth and should NEVER be planned to be used. Traffic holding, weather allowances and alternate fuel are all examples of the legally required fuel above and beyond that needed to drive the aircraft from A to B. Companies will frequently have their own 'Fuel Policy', approved by the aviation regulator, to cover other contingencies that may be particularly relevant to their operation. Accordingly, it makes sense for every pilot in command to establish their own personal 'Fuel Policy' to cover their own unique set of contingencies which may be as simple as their own lack of experience or familiarity with the destination. Essentially, one should always remember that there is legal and there is prudent.

Catering for "reasonably fathomable eventualities" introduces the element of personal judgement into the calculations. It calls for the need to assess what could realistically happen on this flight that may call for additional fuel, even if it isn't LEGALLY required. It is a very broad agenda that will become clearer with experience. These considerations can include single runway destinations; what will I do if an aircraft becomes disabled on the runway? Strong, gusty winds are forecast for the arrival, so the chance of a go-around is very real; how much fuel will that require? At airfields like Los Angeles, the missed approach sends you significantly out to sea before being able to turn back to the field and attempt to regain a slot in the landing sequence. All the time the fuel is being guzzled at low level where the engines are most inefficient.

Icing levels, extensive arrival procedures, avoiding weather enroute and even migratory fruit bats at dusk can all be reasons to consider the carriage of additional fuel above what is dictated by consumption rates, regulatory requirements and company fuel policy. Identify the potential hazards for the particular sector and devise a contingency plan, be it hold for 15 minutes, go-around or divert to another airfield. Then calculate how much fuel this will realistically require. This process not only offers a buffer in terms of fuel, but actively calls for the pilot to make a genuine risk assessment of the sector. If the weather is fine and the destination is a multi-runway equipped airport with a mass of navaids, you may be comfortable with the bare legally required fuel load. But remember, the minute that the plan ceases to proceed exactly to plan, the Variable Reserve is being eroded and very soon a critical fuel situation may be looming, so have a plan in place. Fuel equals time, which equals options.

In Your Hands.

Where fuel is concerned, the buck stops with the pilot-in-command. In airline operations, such things as the check for contaminants and the correct grade of fuel being loaded may be signed over to trained engineers. Even so, the fuel load, its cross-check and assuring that the delegated tasks have been completed still rests with the crew. For the greater majority, all of these tasks fall to the lone individual.

To this end, always allow sufficient time for pre-flight planning and ideally supervise refuelling whenever possible. Ensure well in advance that fuel will be available at your ports of call and that you have the correct means of payment at hand. Visually confirming quantities, the security of fuel caps and checking contaminants are all tasks which can sometimes be easier said than done on cold wet nights, but they are tasks that simply must be done. Fuel and oil are the aircraft's life-blood and should be thought of as such with a corresponding level of importance.

The compromise between fuel uplift and payload or passengers will always exist. As pilot-in-command, the responsibility for a correctly loaded aircraft with sufficient fuel falls to you. Forewarn passengers well in advance of their baggage allowance, explaining the reasons why there is a limit and that it is in the interest of safety that the limit is applied. If payload is critical, then it may simply mean that the planned fuel cannot be uplifted and an additional fuel stop may need to be scheduled.

The initiative and strength to exercise genuine command of fuel management are essential for the safe conduct of flight and in keeping with the spirit of airmanship. Passengers place an immense amount of faith in the pilot, who is often a total stranger. Whether a private pilot or a commercial airline captain, that faith must be respected and repaid with dedication to the task.

At Runway's End.

By the time the engines are brought to life, the flight's fuel planning should form a concise summary on the flight plan. Even so, weather can deteriorate at a destination subsequent to the planning stage, or the activation of restricted airspace can lead to amended routing and additional track miles. Whatever the eventuality, its impact upon fuel management must be considered in a timely manner.

The issues may be covered by a personal 'fuel policy' and simply erode the buffers that have been allowed. However, if those buffers have not been incorporated, the fuel on board may not be sufficient in either a prudent or legal sense. Either way, there will be times when returning to the fuelling station and possibly offloading passengers or freight may be the only option.

On most occasions, the plan will take effect without change and the flight will be underway. At engine start, fuel management remained with us, but transformed from pure planning to a state of active execution. From now until shutdown at the destination, the monitoring of fuel and the myriad of variables will become a central component of safe flight management.

Points to Remember.

* Thoroughly understand the fuel system of your aircraft.

* Recognise that there are legal minimum requirements of fuel carriage, but pilots need to consider the fuel needed for additional contingencies.

* Fuel = Time = Options.

* Fuel is a critical element when considering weight and balance calculations.

CHAPTER FIFTEEN

Fuel for Thought.

In-Flight

Beyond the briefing room, flight planning and calculations, the practical management of fuel becomes a critical component of flight. Despite all of the best intentions, aircraft ranging from biplanes to Boeings have still been forced back to earth prior to their destination because of the mismanagement of fuel.

On the Numbers.

On the completion of flight planning, the fuel status of the flight is generally summarised. Contained within this summary is everything from the predicted fuel burn and 'reserves' to air traffic control and weather requirements. The summary serves to show not only the total fuel on board, but also critically, the fuel margin in excess of requirements. Expressed in units of quantity as well as time, the fuel summary is the starting point for executing a 'fuel plan' in flight.

To apply the fuel summary practically, it should be further simplified as a 'fuel log' and always on hand in the cockpit. The fuel log should be simple, clear, concise and obvious. Its format will often be determined by the complexity of the aircraft and its fuel system, but in the majority of cases starts with the endurance expressed in time. This total time can be further broken down into its distribution across the aircraft's tanks. As such the total endurance may be represented as simply as left and right to reflect two wing tanks, or a series of boxes to represent main and auxiliary tanks. Whatever layout is chosen, keep it logical and orientated. (For example, big boxes for main tanks and smaller boxes for auxiliaries.)

At engine start, log the time and progressively log the fuel remaining and time as fuel tanks are changed in flight. The goal being that the remaining endurance and its distribution in the tanks can be EASILY obtained at any time in flight. Should there be an emergency, or merely a diversion, retrospectively calculating a fuel log is not only potentially distracting but can be prone to error.

A fuel log does not have to be complex. It need only be very basic, expressed in terms of time and understood by the pilot. Legibility is also a factor as small or scrappy logs will make logging the fuel status a significantly more difficult exercise on those wet, dark and turbulent nights.

Set to Go.

The planning is complete, the fuel log is done and we are now ready to fly; or are we? Physically confirming the quantity and the quality of the fuel in the tanks is an important aspect of pre-flight duties and sometimes this is not the easiest task. It may involve climbing a ladder to see right into the tank and dipping it, or endeavouring to confirm the colour of fuel by torch light. Inconvenient and time consuming, they are duties that cannot be rushed or overlooked.

Nor can they be delegated. In airline operations, licensed engineers may oversee the refuelling process and sign for its receipt, but even so, the flight crew will mathematically confirm the stated fuel on board. For refuelling operations, the phrase "trust no-one" comes to mind. A student pilot should always physically verify the aircraft's fuel status and not take the instructor's word as gospel. If there is doubt or confusion, raise the issue and seek clarification on the ground before engine start. Cockpits are not the place for egos, they are the place for co-operation and cross-checking.

Additionally, during the pre-flight inspection it is vital that the hardware of the fuel system is checked and found to be in order. Fuel vents maintain the integrity of the tank and fuel flow through the changes in air pressure with altitude and any blockage can lead to significant problems. Just like pitot tubes and static ports, the vents should always be clear of obstructions.

Look for signs of leaks around tank edges and most importantly, ensure fuel cap security. This can be a tricky task as a cap may appear to be sitting almost flush, but has not actually seated properly. If the cap is difficult to secure, doesn't look 'quite right' or has an uncomfortable degree of movement when in place, remove it and try again. If the situation cannot be rectified, seek out an engineer to discuss the problem. Flight with an ill-fitting fuel cap can lead to suction surreptitiously siphoning fuel into the airflow. Always consider airflow when securing the fuel cap. For those caps with an integral fold down lever, always position the hinge of the lever toward the leading edge so that the airflow doesn't stand a chance of getting under the lever and lifting it.

Where fuel is concerned, there is no room for short cuts and any aspect that can be checked on the ground should be done so thoroughly. Once airborne, the potential consequences of oversight are far greater, so it is vital that the pre-flight inspection is a genuine process, not a just a required formality.

Fuel for Flight.

In flight fuel management commences at engine start. Operating manuals may well dictate which tanks are to be utilised for engine start, but for light aircraft with two wing tanks the simple phrase of "left or least" is often a good starting point. It establishes an easy to remember routine that will check the serviceability of one tank during the taxi phase. Engine start provides an opportunity to note the function of 'boost pumps', and following start, note the time and the selected tank on the fuel log. Prior to engine run-up, change tanks to the fullest tank and log it, thereby confirming the operation of both tanks before the wheels ever leave the runway. For aircraft with mains, auxiliaries and cross feeds, a similar routine can be established to confirm the serviceability of varying tank configurations prior to flight.

Established in the cruise, all pilots have a cycle of activity that they attend to encompassing varying aspects from navigation to confirming aircraft performance. Part of this process may involve 'leaning the mixture'. This is significant to fuel management as the fuel plan has been calculated using a specific cruise fuel consumption. In turn, leaning the mixture may be required to achieve this consumption rate and a failure to do so will invalidate the projected fuel plan and critically, reduce the endurance. Furthermore, it is generally advisable to be established in the cruise before further varying tank selections, though there will be some situations where this is not the case. Changing tanks can serve to maintain symmetry between wing tanks or vary the centre of gravity of an aeroplane as the available fuel is accessed. Identify the strategy that is applicable to your particular aircraft and operation.

For single engine aircraft, changing tanks should be carefully considered. While tank symmetry is an issue, the availability of a forced landing field below may well determine the location to change tanks and represent another reason for planning a flight route over friendly terrain and enroute airfields. Healthy aviation pessimism would have the pilot consider what would happen if the selector broke off in my hand at this point. In the worst case the engine stops and the best case, only the remaining fuel in one tank is accessible. Either way, the option of a potential landing field below is a prudent aspect of planning in changing tanks.

For multi-engined aircraft, prudence would suggest that the changing of tanks be 'staggered' to a degree to avoid both engines going silent simultaneously. Ensure that the new fuel selection is successfully established for a few minutes before repeating the process for the other engine.

For all aircraft, the key to fuel management is a methodical, unrushed approach. Consider the procedure involved, the current situation and fuel status. When satisfied with all aspects, execute the procedure by confirming each step before actioning. That the fuel quantity is adequate, that the fuel pressure is stable, that the selector is the correct lever and so on. At each step, pause slightly and confirm what has just occurred. Also, be very wary of distractions. Luck will always have it that a radio call or a talkative passenger will pull your attention away from the task at hand at the critical moment. Completing the fuel log *only* when the tank selection process is absolutely completed can serve as another defence against oversight.

Night flying can introduce another set of variables. What is obvious by day may escape the attention by night unless a degree of vigilance is maintained. One example of this is venting fuel. By day, the streaming mist of atomised fuel from a fuel cap or breather vent will often catch the attention of the pilot. By night, the crew must be proactive and periodically shine a torch or illuminate 'wing lights' to ensure that no such event is taking place. Similarly, the poor lighting in many cockpits call for extra care and illumination to verify the action when moving fuel selectors.

By day or night, on successful completion of the process and the fuel log, use the opportunity to reassess the aircraft's fuel status and remaining endurance. Plan ahead for when the next tank change may occur. Possibly seek the latest weather for your destination and if a diversion was called for now, where is the nearest airfield and what are the fuel requirements? Similarly, when waypoints call for the completion of the flight log, they should also prompt an overall cycle of activity in the cockpit which includes a review of the aircraft's fuel situation. Fuel equals time and time equals options.

Not to Plan.

The nature of aviation is closely related to the phrase involving the "best laid plans of mice and men". Despite meticulous planning and attention to detail, the dynamic environment of aviation can mean that things may not always go to plan. Whenever plans change, fuel management becomes a prime consideration. Planned winds can be unreliable, diversions around weather can occur or flight at a lower level may be necessary and all can erode valuable fuel stocks.

The nature of the disruption may be a technical issue such as an engine failure which calls for specific management of fuel, perhaps accessing fuel from one wing tank to supply the engine on the opposite side; or 'cross-feeding'. More often though, the disruption will be a change in routing, a diversion or perhaps flight at a lower level where the engines are thirstier. Whatever the nature of the change, it needs to be considered in terms of fuel and thereby in terms of time.

Time permitting, when an event arises that might change your plans, it is always handy to note the time beside your fuel log. When the situation is under control, consider the impact upon fuel consumption rates, ground speed, range and endurance of the current situation. This may be the case if an engine has been shut down on a twin engine aircraft.

Should the need arise for a diversion or increased holding requirements due to changing weather at the destination, a recalculation of the available fuel and fuel required will be necessary. In the midst of some of these relatively complex calculations, it is worthwhile to work out a 'master time' for the purposes of your planning. This may be the latest time at which you can divert and still reach your alternate with the legally required fuel, or it may be as simple as the latest time that you need to be back on the ground with minimum reserves. Always be conservative in assessing the fuel remaining on board and err on the high side when considering fuel consumption. Then, note the 'master time' boldly in a prominent position near the fuel log. Throughout the process always remember to aviate, navigate and communicate. Do not get head down and lost solely in the calculation; always fly the aircraft first.

Re-planning in flight is merely the nature of aviation and like every aspect of this field of endeavour, a developed strategy is a great asset. When a fuel strategy is concerned remember to be conservative, methodical and consider options in terms of time.

Down to Earth.

Having ensured that the fuel system is appropriately configured for the approach and landing, the flight is successfully concluded and the aircraft is shutdown. However, there are still some post flight duties involved with fuel management.

Firstly, complete your fuel log and compare this to your *planned* arrival fuel. In turn, it is worthwhile to dip the tanks and compare the actual fuel remaining with your calculated figure. Some operations will require this figure to be logged on aircraft or company documentation. Furthermore, dipping the tanks after flight can reveal a lot about both flight planning and fuel consumption. This is highly valuable information for the next time you plan to fly the aircraft and in rare cases may expose unserviceabilities such as a fuel leak.

Such attention to detail post-flight is indicative of the overall attitude that should be afforded to fuel management. Simply put, fuel is the aircraft's lifeblood and without it, it will cease to function. As the pilot in command it is imperative that fuel is properly managed from flight planning to after engine shutdown. Far fewer incidents and accidents would occur if this responsibility was exercised with the due diligence that it deserves.

The critical importance of fuel management cannot be over-emphasised. It is a core component in the conduct of safe powered flight and should be treated as such. Whenever aviation is involved, there should always be fuel for thought.

Points to Remember.

* Preferably, fuel logs should be simple, logical and easy to understand.

* Regularly monitor your fuel status and its progress compared to the original flight plan.

* When any aspect of a flight changes, consider its impact upon fuel management.

* Always assess your fuel status after the flight and compare it to the original plan.

CHAPTER SIXTEEN

MANAGING IN-FLIGHT EMERGENCIES

The degree and nature of emergencies can vary in scale to a huge degree. There may be a sick passenger who requires medical attention, or the aircraft itself could be compromised due to a technical issue. Regardless of the problem, it is a situation that requires attention, yet it must not distract from the overall safety of the aircraft. In the past, airliners have crashed when the crew has become focussed on a small problem at the expense of actually flying the aeroplane.

Preparation Before Perspiration.

One of the best assets in dealing with an emergency is being adequately prepared. In some cases, that involves knowing the aircraft's systems, limitations and emergency actions before even leaving the ground. No-one expects a pilot to know every single detail about every aircraft they fly, but certain core numbers and procedures should be learned. When the lone engine of a light aircraft fails, there is not time to refer to the manuals to recall the best glide speed or immediate actions. Also in the planning stages, enroute airports and terrain can be considered should a diversion or expedited landing become necessary.

However, being prepared extends beyond acquiring a level of knowledge and pre-flight planning. Preparation is a dynamic skill that takes place constantly through each and every flight. In between admiring the wonderful view from aloft I always ask myself, "What would I do now if…?" The scenario can be varied to cater for a range of situations. "What would I do now if I had a fire on board?", "What would I do now if the engine fails?" "What would I do now if I start leaking fuel? The list is seemingly endless.

In some cases, such as an engine failure in a 'single', if you have to look once the engine has failed, then you may have left it a little late. Some years ago, while conducting a student's pre-licence test, we suffered an engine failure and carried out a forced landing in less than ideal terrain. Having an awareness of potential landing fields prior to the engine failure was critical to the successful outcome.

It is a routine that is neither designed to make a flight laborious nor induce panic and perhaps only one or two questions need to be asked on any particular flight. However, it is a valuable exercise that can cover a good many potential emergencies over time. It calls upon the actions that need to be taken to deal with the emergency and then how the flight should be subsequently managed. "Where will I go?" "Do I need to land NOW, divert or can I continue to my destination?"

To make the best decisions, it is imperative that the pilot always maintains a level of "situational awareness", or S.A. Situational awareness is an appreciation of the current situation in terms of time, space and surroundings and being able to project forward to where the aircraft will be in the immediate future. Understanding the terrain below, the airfields nearby and the weather ahead are all aspects of being situationally aware, just as understanding what is their significance, should an engine fail at any given moment.

Having this "mental picture" of where the aircraft is in space relative to its options and 'escape plans' BEFORE an emergency occurs is a tremendous advantage. For when an emergency arises, the startle factor will release the adrenalin and the brain will initially struggle to keep pace as multiple inputs call for processing. Being situationally aware beforehand initially unloads the brain of one task temporarily.

The Urgency of an Emergency.

At first glance, urgency and emergency would seem to complement each other in both rhyme and intent. However, haste is waste is probably a more applicable turn of phrase. An emergency certainly requires attention, but the pace at which it needs to be addressed depends on the nature of the problem. If an engine fails in a single-engined aircraft, gravity will dictate that the best glide speed is achieved without delay, but even then, an engine failure at 8,000 feet is very different from an engine failure at 800 feet. Also, a 'rough running' engine that is still producing power may need very careful management to nurse it to a nearby airport. A rushed flurry of hands and feet and pushing and pulling of levers without careful thought could lead to the situation becoming far worse.

Time can be a difficult dance partner when an emergency takes place. It can be a limiting factor as fuel and altitude are finite commodities. Furthermore, our perception of time can be altered when we are under the stress of an emergency. As we venture down a line of action, time and fuel may be unsuspectingly consumed as we fly further away from our destination. When an emergency first takes place, noting down the time, fuel on board and starting a timer can be a handy tool to assist our ongoing situational awareness and planning.

The conundrum we are faced with in an emergency is that time is precious and yet we should not rush. What we need to do is use our available time efficiently and that stems from being organised and having a plan.

AVIATE –NAVIGATE –COMMUNICATE.

In any situation, be it an emergency or simply managing a distraction, in the first instance we should aviate, navigate and communicate (ANC).

'Aviate' calls for the pilot to keep the aircraft flying. Do not allow the airspeed to erode to the point of stall, or enter a spiral dive with increasing airspeed and load factor upon the aircraft. Keeping the aircraft under positive control is the first priority as all other issues become secondary should that control be lost.

'Navigate' calls for the pilot to put the aircraft in a safe place. With 'aviate' taken care of and the aircraft flying safely, the pilot needs to keep the aircraft clear of terrain and adverse weather.

'Communicate' is the third component of this important trilogy, but does sit in a fairly distant third place. Becoming engrossed in radio communications in a critical situation can be dangerously distracting and can erode the ability to 'aviate' and 'navigate'. However, it may be worth making a brief initial call to alert air traffic control and other aircraft of your situation. In a high traffic environment, this may allow the controller to begin clearing an airborne path and alerting ground services for you while you deal with the emergency.

Whether the call is an urgent 'Mayday' or just an advisory call, attaching the words, "…standby further" to the end of the radio transmission can be very useful. Often the controllers first response will be to ask how many people are on board, how much fuel do you have and are there any dangerous goods on board? They are all valid questions that can be answered at an appropriate time. The first transmission is YOUR transmission to relay YOUR situation and location. Keep it brief, return to aviating and navigating and offer further details when time permits. "Standby!" is a powerful word and allows you to retain control of the communication.

We have aviated, navigated and communicated – now it is time for a plan.

Making a Plan.

As mentioned earlier, a general plan for some emergencies can be considered before flight and definitely before the emergency takes place. There are many techniques taught relating to how to deal with emergencies, however, no single template can ever cover all situations. Consequently, having a flexible process that can be adapted depending on the event or time available is a worthwhile method.

Like a broken record, Aviate – Navigate – Communicate should come first. With the aircraft under control and in a 'safe place' we need to diagnose the problem and unfortunately sometimes that can be more easily said than done. Unusual noises and vibrations can sometimes be very distracting but the aircraft may actually still be maintaining power, height and airspeed. A timely landing may be advisable. Other issues may be more obvious, but still it can be unwise to leap into assumptions.

See if there are other supporting items of evidence. Is the low oil pressure supported by high oil temperature? If the tachometer is reading zero but the engine is still loud and strong and there has been no loss of performance, perhaps you may consider an instrument failure.

When you have diagnosed the problem, apply the checklist that is appropriate. Some may be needed to be recalled from memory in urgent situations, while others may permit reference to a checklist or manual. As you do this, check back...aviate - navigate - communicate.... always keep the aircraft safe and flying.

Once you have the aircraft flying safely with your checklists and drills complete, it is time to make a decision. Bearing in mind, if an obviously safe option exists such as a nearby airfield, it would be wise to turn towards this in the initial 'navigate' phase before you commence your checklists. As mentioned in the chapter "Decisions, Decisions", there are numerous ways of coming to a decision and numerous factors affecting the subsequent plan of action. Whichever, method you may choose, it is imperative to make that decision, take action and then review the plan once it is underway.

Monitor the Situation.

Just as it is important to review a course of action, it is crucial that the original emergency is monitored. Whether it is a deterioration of weather, a fuel leak or an engine vibration, it is imperative to continually assess the current status of the situation. Should the situation become worse, it may well be that your initial plan needs to be revised to land the aircraft sooner.

Furthermore, the signs and symptoms of an ailing aircraft can sometimes be very subtle. A low vibration may just be an early symptom of a greater problem that takes some time to manifest on the instrumentation. I have personally had a very low airframe vibration that only became critical when the flaps were selected and the power setting changed on approach. The culprit was discovered to be a bird-strike that I was totally unaware of.

To assist in monitoring, it is always worthwhile to keep a 'log' of the event. Just as we monitor our fuel usage and fuel on board against the clock, when some form of emergency occurs in flight and the situation permits, write down the time, the fuel on board and in a few words, what has taken place. When a change takes place, note the time again and the new information in a few words. This can assist in trouble-shooting but it can also tangibly reaffirm that a situation is deteriorating, prompting further action.

Safe and Sound?

You have flown the aircraft safely, monitored the situation and now you have landed at your chosen airfield. But, the job is not quite over.

Firstly, until the aircraft is stationary and with all occupants clear of the aircraft, there is still the potential for problems. Over the years, landing gear has unexpectedly collapsed and strange odours have escalated rapidly into a fire, so don't let your guard down now. As part of your pre-flight briefing you should have prepared the passengers for disembarking and doing so quickly in an emergency. Additionally, prior to the landing, any further required actions on landing such as assuming the 'Brace' position or evacuating should've been covered. On leaving the aircraft, continue to take responsibility for your passengers, marshalling them to a safe distance from the aircraft. It is important to remain aware of your surroundings as you don't want to safely return to Mother Earth, only to have a passenger stray onto an active runway or taxiway. If the emergency allowed you to park the aircraft in a normal fashion, still care for your passengers and it is worthwhile to discuss the events of the flight with them to put them at ease.

As always, there will be paperwork to complete after an inflight event. There may be safety reports to file and aircraft logs to fill in. It is critical that you also enter any relevant details in the Maintenance

Release as this is the document that should both initiate attention from engineering and prevent any subsequent flight until the fault 'signed off'.

Expect the Unexpected.

Inflight emergencies are something that we hope never happen, but that we need to be prepared for. There is no hard and fast rule book as no two emergencies are ever the same. To manage the situation to the best of your ability you need to be well prepared before you leave the ground, always keep the aircraft flying safely and in a safe place and then methodically work through the problem. The time, daylight, altitude and/or fuel available will sometimes dictate the pace at which this occurs, but an organised process is still the best method to ensure that the key items are not overlooked.

It is worth remembering that there will be an initial 'startle factor' and adrenalin rush. This may feel like a wave of panic and a few stunned seconds may follow – this is natural human reaction. Take a breath, allow the pilot to rise up, remember your training and start the process with aviate – navigate – communicate.

Aviation is full of challenges and in some ways that is why we enjoy it so much. Some of those challenges occur every flight, while some may occur once in a lifetime. Regardless of the frequency, we are obliged to maintain our skills and always be prepared. It may take an hour here or there to study, or a few minutes in flight to review our options. However, this will be time very well spent when seconds may count.

Points to Remember.

* One of the best assets in dealing with an emergency is being adequately prepared.

* Time can be a critical factor when an emergency takes place.

* Some emergencies are slow to arise and insidious in nature. Monitor them carefully from the first indication and formulate a plan.

* Avoid the inevitable distractions of an emergency and fly the aircraft as a priority. Aviate – Navigate – Communicate.

CHAPTER SEVENTEEN

FLYING WITH FRIENDS

One of the great aspects of being a pilot is being able to share the experience with friends and family. To take them aloft in our three dimensional world and show them an entirely new perspective is a wonderful privilege filled with personal satisfaction and excitement. However, herein lies the lurking threats and subtle pressures that can impinge on safety.

In the Beginning.

Regardless of whether an operation is private or commercial or the 'payload' is close friends or air freight, being the pilot-in-command comes with the associated responsibilities. They shouldn't be thought of as a burden, but just an aspect of airmanship that you can be proud of. You've worked hard for your licence and your professional approach will actually demonstrate to your passengers what is involved in conveying people safely by air. In this age of locked flight decks and security checks, there are very few opportunities to allow the greater public to see what is involved 'behind the scenes', so this is your chance.

Time can be your friend or your enemy. If you leave everything until the last minute on the day of the flight, then you've invited unnecessary pressure into the process. Well in advance of the flight, you can convey certain points to your passengers such as the need for punctuality and the potential for weather to interfere with even the best laid plans. Nominate a time to meet well before the scheduled departure to allow for traffic hiccups and preserving an adequate time for briefing.

So often the weather can be the frustrating variable in the equation. Still, if you have given your passengers adequate notice and a simple explanation of the requirements in advance, it can ease last-minute disappointment. There will still be disappointment, but very few passengers will argue when you commence any aviation-related sentence with, "In the interests of safety…" Years ago I used to fly in an early morning commercial operation to an airfield that did not possess any navigation aids or an instrument approach. However, it did possess copious amounts of fog and hills, which is never a great combination.

Before each flight I would advise them that in the "interests of safety" we may divert enroute to a major airport without fog. They could hire a car from there and I could bring the aircraft over to them when the fog cleared. I gave them the option to cancel the flight or accept a safe option, this both laid out the facts to them and removed any undue pressure from me to fly to the original destination. If the fog cleared, then that was a bonus. I never had a single complaint and our company remained their first choice for all of their flying needs.

Having allowed time for your passengers to be briefed, it is ideal that you attend to as many of your duties as possible prior to their arrival. Firstly, always confirm that the aircraft is available and serviceable with a valid Maintenance Release. Flight plan submission, paperwork, refuelling and a pre-flight inspection are all tasks that are best achieved without waiting passengers potentially creating time pressure. Haste does not live well with aviation and when rushing a pre-flight inspection or something similar, it is an opportunity to overlook a critical task. Make time your ally not your enemy. It is also worthwhile to ensure that the aircraft is nicely presented and ready to go before you move to greet your passengers. 'Dressing' the harnesses, cleaning the windscreens, fitting headsets, cleaning out rubbish and ensuring that all seats have sick bags are all additional tasks that are best done in advance.

Furthermore, once your passengers arrive, they will need your attention. They will possibly be unfamiliar with light aircraft and you will need to be with them at every point. You may even have to remind them to go to the toilet as there isn't a bathroom in a 4-seater! That reminder can form part of your pre-flight briefing where you can point out other elements such as where you will be flying, for how long and certain points of interest along the way. This will peak their interest and minimise questions in the air when you may be too busy to answer. The time to fly is now approaching.

Pilot-In-Command.

They are your friends and family, but you are still the pilot-in-command and responsible for their safety. As you leave the confines of the flight office, they are entering an alien world of spinning propellers, protruding pitot tubes and tail rotors. Keep them close and keep them safe. Reaffirm the "Don't Touch" policy and if they wish to take photos, stop and supervise as walking backwards to get a shot in frame can end very badly at an airport.

On arrival at the aircraft, walk them around introduce them to some basic components as this also offers another opportunity to briefly revalidate the full pre-flight inspection that you created earlier. Before boarding, secure any baggage or freight and always highlight the "No Step" areas.

On board and before the noise of the engine commences, take the time to run through the function of the seat belts and doors. Have them actually fasten and unfasten, open and close, as committing the action is far more easily remembered than a verbal instruction. Let them know that you are happy to answer questions but not during take-off and landing unless you give the OK and not if you are on the radio, when you may choose to raise your hand indicating they should pause. You can also tell them your call-sign should they be listening out and enlist their eyes-in-the-sky to alert you to any other traffic they may spot. Occasionally it will be a Boeing 747 that is 20,000 feet above you, but that's ok – thank and encourage them.

The use of cameras can be discussed, particularly the use of flashes, and the stowage of hand luggage so it doesn't impede the controls or the egress. For aerobatics, zippered pockets are a must to prevent coins and even small items coming loose in flight.

It is also at this time that an emergency briefing regarding belts, exits and life jackets is very worthwhile in a calm, measured voice. It is also an idea to reassure the passengers that you don't anticipate an emergency, but should one occur today, you have been trained and it is best to discuss it now in an unhurried manner. Ask if there are any questions too as there is still a convenient opportunity for the nervous flyer to opt out and remain on the ground.

It may sound rather formal for a leisurely flight with friends, but the nature of aviation is such that it calls for a level of professionalism regardless of the level of operation. You can be pleasant, but you are in command and cannot be drawn into the frivolity that my stem from the excitement. It can be distracting and doesn't give the passengers a suitable frame of reference for the person that is about to take their lives into the sky. Additionally, should the frivolity get so boisterous that it compromises any aspect of the flight, you should exert appropriate assertion as the pilot-in-command to return the mood to a safe level. This can be done in a calm, friendly manner and your passengers deserve nothing less.

Flight of a Lifetime.

For some of your friends and family, the flight will be the experience of a lifetime. Something that they will remember fondly, share on social media and discuss with others for years to come. So it's in everyone's interest for the flight to be safe and comfortable.

In the air, interact with your passengers without becoming distracted. If someone is feeling ill, ensure that there is adequate ventilation and restate the availability of sick bags. Sometimes passengers can ease their nausea if you offer them a map and set them the task of spotting a feature, as this occupies their thoughts and the repetition of the droning engine seems to fade into the background. If a passenger does become very ill, or even extremely panicked, to the degree that you need to return, then focus on flying the aircraft. Don't panic or rush, as no-one benefits when the overall safety of the flight is compromised.

As you approach landmarks of note, let your passengers know so that they can ready their cameras. There may be the ability to fly an orbit to allow the shots to be taken. In this case, consider whether the aircraft is a high wing or low wing and where is the sun relative to the aircraft? As always, fly the aircraft first and foremost.

It's Not Over Yet.

As you return towards the airport, remind your passengers that things will become busy soon and you won't be able to chat as the radio requirements and traffic become busier. You may have pointed out the flaps on that walk around the aircraft before flight and they may see these being lowered on approach. Also, an advanced warning of the landing gear locking down can be beneficial.

Having landed and shutdown, your passengers remain your responsibility until you return them to the flight office. Complete your checklists and log your maintenance times as required and then escort your passengers from the tarmac as you did on their arrival. While you still have post flight responsibilities as a pilot, take the time to savour the moment once the task is completed and the keys and paperwork have been returned to the flight office.

Now there is an opportunity to relive the flight with your friends and share in their excitement. You have kept them safe and given them a glimpse of a very special world. You should be proud and they will be thankful and respectful of your attention to detail, even if they don't always say it. Leisure flights don't allow the pilot to be 'leisurely', but being organised and professional needn't erode the enjoyment and can in fact enhance the experience by nullifying potential items of stress. No matter how many hours you accumulate over the years, one of the great joys will always remain the ability to fly with family and friends.

Points to Remember.

* Passengers are the responsibility of the pilot, both in the air and on the ground.

* Avoid the pressures of time and disappointed passengers by arriving early and keeping passengers informed.

* Aircraft and airports can be a dangerous environment for passengers. Brief them and supervise accordingly.

* The phrase, "In the interests of safety…" can be a useful tool when explaining certain requirements of a flight to passengers.

CHAPTER EIGHTEEN

THE VALUE OF CURRENCY

So often the issue of experience is paramount in a pilot's career. Total flight time, experience on type and multi-engine hours are all barometers used to assess a pilot's possible expertise. While a valid means of measurement in one sense, an equally critical aspect in the present tense is the matter of currency.

Keeping it Relevant.

The log book tells the story of our journey along the path of aviation. We carefully log each hour and eventually the next personal goal draws nearer. Ultimately when standards are met and qualifications are gained the log book continues to tick over, day by day, and reflects the overall experience of the pilot.

Yet within the log book's story are a number of smaller chapters. They relate not only how much experience was gained, but the nature of the flight and the time that has lapsed since. This gives weight to the relevance of the experience. 10,000 hours in command of a Boeing 747 won't necessarily equate to a safe crop-dusting pilot weaving amongst the trees and power lines. Nor will a little crop-dusting experience in the distant past ready a pilot to depart today for a low level spraying run without some type of refresher training.

Within commercial operations a thorough record is kept of the last instrument approach, night landing and so on to meet the regulatory requirements. By virtue of the full time nature of the employment, recency is not generally an issue. Even so, in the summer months with long days, night landings can prove elusive and for Check Captains confined to simulators and observing from 'jump seats', actual flying can be of a premium. Even seasoned campaigners need to be wary of a lack of currency.

It's not Easy.

Flight time needs to be relevant and this can at times provide a real challenge. With the cost of flying providing a challenge at the best of times, it is genuinely difficult for the private pilot to keep their 'hand in' at all. The vast majority of licensed private pilots struggle to fly 50 hours per annum, or less than an hour each week. As such, when they do become airborne, it is vital that the maximum value is extracted from the time aloft.

While the minimum requirements may call three take-offs and landings every 90 days, is this really adequate? Furthermore, this may only be a requirement for the carriage of passengers. And what of the prevailing conditions? There are no stipulations regarding crosswinds, exposure to controlled airspace or runway length. A pilot may have satisfied the minimum requirements at a home port before launching solo through controlled airspace to a short, unsealed airstrip with a howling crosswind. Sure, a flight school may have additional requirements for hiring an aircraft, but what about the private owner? There is legal and then there is prudent.

Having conducted a number of Biennial Flight Reviews (BFR) in the past, it can be quite interesting to see the varying standards of operation amongst pilots. However, the core problem was often an issue of recency and sheer lack of practice. The pilots had managed to maintain their 3 take-offs and landings, but little else. There had been no practiced forced landings, go-arounds, flapless or short field operations since their last review; and it showed.

As I have said, I sympathise and can even empathise with the reality of economics that can make every minute aloft financially painful; however, there is still a duty of care to ourselves, our passengers, other airspace users and those folks whose homes we fly over. As such, we must all shoulder the responsibility and make every effort to be as proficient as possible before we utter the words, "Clear Prop!"

Putting a Plan in Place.

A successful flight at all levels of aviation is the culmination of not only manipulative skills but sound planning. Frequently, the level of preparation I have witnessed for private pilot licence flight tests has been phenomenal, with pre-flight planning endeavouring to account for any number of variables that may surface along the way. Unfortunately, once the licence has been gained that state of readiness is often eroded by a combination of factors ranging from currency to complacency.

While 'risk management' is in danger of becoming a trendy catch-cry, it is actually a worthy way of thinking about staying safe in the face of infrequent flying. Well in advance of a flight, sit back in the comfort of your home and honestly consider which aspects of the sortie give you a sense of unease or trepidation. What bad experiences have you had previously? Were you confronted with a late runway change, or flared far too high on landing? Were you high on approach or did you get lost on some poorly signed taxiways? These areas can be a great place to start.

Re-assess the difficulty you encountered on the previous occasion and how it may have been avoided. Slowing down earlier and selecting flap may have offered some breathing space, reviewing the taxiways before engine start may have saved some confusion. Whatever the issue, consider the risk and mitigate against it. As always, rehearsing by 'armchair flying' can offer a great means of mentally preparing for busy phases of the flight. If it's good enough for aerobatic champions and Red Bull Air Race pilots, then it's good enough for us mere mortals.

Also, review the flight ahead, just as if it was a flight test. Consider not only the operational perspective, but the procedural items and aim to get those calls and checklists just right. Re-visit the handling notes for your aeroplane and ensure that the crucial numbers are in your head. If flights are few and far between, use the opportunity to brush up on any changes that may have occurred in the intervening period and a chat with a flight instructor could be worth its weight in gold. Furthermore, it is vital to make every minute count when the meter is running. That is not to say that the flight should be all hard work, but it should be productive as well as enjoyable.

Making the Most of the Minutes.

The aircraft is booked and the home preparation is complete. Arrive at the airfield early and avoid rushing as haste often walks hand in hand with oversight and omission. Use the pre-flight inspection as an opportunity to revisit the various components and limitations of your aeroplane; flaps and limit speeds, fuel tanks and capacity and consumption.

With all of the ground aspects covered, the time has come to maximise the benefit of the actual flight. While there is great satisfaction to be found in the safe carriage of passengers, ensure that adequate flights are planned to be flown solo. Solo flight facilitates the ability to conduct exercises such as glide approaches and also permits full concentration without the potential distraction and added responsibility of passengers.

Rather than a mere series of take offs and landings, plan a flight that encompasses as many tasks as possible. Once you have committed to going flying and you are paying for start-up and taxi time, there is actual value in extending the flight a little more to maximise the content. Too often certain manoeuvres only see the light of day at periodic reviews. They should be flown to enhance handling and a pleasing by-product is a sound state of readiness when the flight review ultimately rolls around again.

The format of a solo session may include a normal departure, then cruising to the training area through a combination of normal, slow and high speed cruise. Perhaps a segment within the white arc with a stage of flap extended as preparation for those circuit situations where a slower preceding aircraft has gone wide in the pattern. Established clear of the circuit area and at a safe height, some steep turns to the left and right, followed by a practice forced landing. Consider your fuel status and consider changing tanks before returning to the circuit via standard joining procedures and flying a mixture of normal, 'short field' and flapless circuits. Make the first one a normal touch and go to re-establish the base line clearly in your mind and make the final landing to full stop a short field approach to remind you how much runway is actually used. And really nail that aim point!

In all sessions practice a go-around. It is a very under-valued manoeuvre that can be called for under any number of circumstances. Even from a perfect approach, a runway incursion can necessitate a go-around, similarly, it is the safest solution to an untidy approach or unsatisfactory landing. If in doubt; bug out! The ability to conduct a safe missed approach is a tremendous ace up the sleeve and should be part of a pilot's armoury at all times.

Such a session as described offers a very good workout; far more so than simply circuits. The individual pilot may wish to bias the format to suit their own areas of weakness, but regardless it should be a rounded exercise in handling and procedures. Such a session can comfortably be achieved in a little over an hour if it is planned in advance and time is not wasted dawdling around the sky wondering what comes next. Make your flying count, it may not be frequent, but it can still be of quality.

True Value.

Even with a genuine effort to maintain relevant, quality currency, skills can erode with time. For this reason, it is a sound investment to fly with a flight instructor periodically to assess your standard and to offer advice. Before the flight, let the instructor know what you wish to achieve from the flight and even present the format that you'd like to fly. Not only will a quality flight be the result, but the fear and loathing of flight reviews will subside.

Private pilots are not the only ones who reap the benefits of a dual check. Highly experienced commercial pilots recognise that the relevance of their current operations may not prepare them ideally to take the family for a leisure flight in a light aircraft. They are the first to recognise the importance of recency and seek the counsel of a youthful instructor with their finger on the relevant pulse.

Much of flying is about enjoyment and this can be greatly enhanced by a degree of confidence and proficiency. Maintaining a level of proficiency is always difficult in the face of the financial challenges, but that being said, it is no excuse for cutting corners. Every flight should be treasured. Plan it thoroughly, maximise the value of the air time and then honestly review your performance once the aircraft has been tied down for the night. These are the hallmarks of a good pilot and the means by which one's standards can improve.

It is one thing to be highly experienced, but just as in life, age is no guarantee of wisdom. Maintaining a quality of skill and airmanship calls for far more than meeting bare legal requirements, it calls for thorough preparation and execution. Being current is not merely a function of dates, take offs and landings. It is a combination of confidence, competence and readiness to cope with all aspects of the impending flight. When this is appreciated, so too is the true value of currency.

Points to Remember.

* For a pilot to feel safe and confident, the prudent level of currency can mean more than the bare legal requirement.

* Recent experience may not always be on a relevant aircraft type.

* Make use of flight time to hone a range of skills.

* A check flight with an instructor can be a tremendous asset, even if it is not legally required.

CHAPTER NINETEEN

THE DANGER OF DISTRACTIONS

At times it can seem like modern life is just one big distraction. Information, communications, sounds and sights bombard us from every angle, potentially skewing our focus from the primary task in front of us. Unfortunately, the same can be said for the modern cockpit and as pilots we need to guard against these potential threats.

Nothing New.

While our high-paced world has brought with it new ways to divert our attention, pilots have always had the potential to be distracted. Some distractions come from outside the aviation realm, while others can be integral such as air traffic control communications. Regardless of the source they can erode the primary task of flying the aircraft.

The size of the aircraft and the number of crew on board are no barrier to distractions. The loss of Eastern Air Lines Flight 401 was a tragedy that stemmed at its core from a crew becoming focussed on a burnt out lightbulb on the flight deck. In trying to resolve the bulb issue they did not notice that they had inadvertently altered the autopilot mode and the aircraft descended into the Florida Everglades. The investigation highlighted a number of issues and the accident led to changes on subsequent airliners and in the study of 'human factors'.

In our light aircraft cockpits there have always been tasks that can draw our attention from flying the aeroplane. Something as simple as looking for a dropped pencil can have us head down and looking at the floor at a critical time if we don't guard against it. A sick passenger, an annoying whistling around the door seal or an intermittent gauge can all catch us off-guard and directing more attention than is warranted and at an inappropriate time. Distractions call for us to be aware, eliminate when possible and prioritise as necessary.

A Brave New World.

Technology can be a double-edged sword. It has filled our aircraft with moving maps and easy-to-read colour displays that present a wealth of information that can detail the aircraft's health and enhance our situational awareness. Such tools in general aviation aircraft were a mere dream not so many years ago, but now they are both commonplace and cost effective.

What we must be wary of is that the technology doesn't draw all our attention within the cockpit. The multiple options at our fingertips possess the temptation to flick between them like changing TV channels while Synthetic Vision Technology (SVT) displays can border on being hypnotic. In visual flight, our primary scan needs to remain outside to assess the weather, traffic and terrain, using the information within the cockpit to support it and not the other way around.

As smartphones, Ipads and other tablets become a part of a pilot's armoury, they also come with a range of operational Apps that can assist us in the conduct of flight. However, they too can become consuming as we have discovered in everyday life use. Worse still, these devices are equipped with almost limitless non-aviation related functions that can divert our valuable attention if we allow this to occur. We have seen how such behaviour has caused carnage on our roads and inattention at altitude can be equally lethal.

The new age has brought with it the rapid sharing of information via the internet and inflight videos are no exception. Increasingly, aviators are using equipment such as Go-Pro cameras to capture the magic of flight and share it with a broader audience. Some of the footage that is available is nothing less than spectacular and we are all privileged to view it. That being said, within the camera fittings and functions are the potential to interfere with the safe operation of flight if we allow the camera to overtake our concentration.

The technology is here to stay and I suspect it will continue to evolve at an incredible rate. Used properly, it serves to benefit us all, however, when used incorrectly we are inviting distractions into our cockpit. As we embrace the technology, we must also be mindful of its management and its proper place in our priorities.

Managing Distractions.

The first step in managing distractions is awareness. Realising that the very technologies that can assist us also have the potential to harm is crucial. Yet, we should not solely focus on the new technologies as we consider awareness as many of our old threats are still lurking.

Considering how we may be challenged before taking flight is key and comes with the relative luxury of time and the comfort of solid ground. Sometimes this will extend beyond assessing the hardware and software needed to fly. Hunger, fatigue, illness and one's personal life can all prove distracting at times. I had the latter occur first hand when my father was terminally ill and in the last weeks of his life. I was flying by day and nursing him by night, but eventually the latter began to erode my focus and physically fatigue me. Ultimately, I stood myself down from flying duties, which was a difficult decision as chief pilot, but my personal life was far to present in the cockpit.

A more common strategy is to lay out the items that you carry in flight and assess them one by one. Whether it be clothing, charts, documents or writing implements, you don't want to be searching for them in flight, so cockpit organisation is important. This can even be honed down to storing the same items in the same compartments of a flight bag each and every time, that way you can find equipment by feel on a dark night. Additionally, items that you may need in flight should be securely stowed and within arm's reach.

With reference to the new technologies, are there brackets, chargers or other supplementary items needed to run the equipment in flight? If so, organise their arrangement in advance. Similarly, if there are cameras, Apps or avionics to be used, become familiar with their operation before using them in flight. The same can be said for some of the advanced instrumentation fit-outs in modern aircraft. A thorough grounding in the system is imperative, not only to minimise distractions, but to maximise the information that can be drawn from it.

It's always enjoyable to drive out to the airfield and wander about the flightline of your flying school or club. This time can also be used very beneficially in managing distractions in advance. When it comes to the aircraft, you can always cast a critical eye over the airframe to highlight potential distractions.

Firstly, consider how you would organise your cockpit given the equipment you have recently reviewed. Where can you mount your tablet, or best stow spare pencils? Then look around and assess other components and there are many. Everything from how to adjust your seat to securing the doors. Consider what action you would take if the door came open on take-off? The radio transceivers, therein lies another threat. Where does answering radio calls rate compared to flying the aeroplane? The windscreen, is it crazed or dirty, will that prove to be a distraction? Passengers can be prone to interrupting at inopportune moments and to the bystander, cutting them off can appear rude. Beforehand, it may be worth briefing that there'll be no chatter in the critical phases of flight and if you have to put up your hand to stop them talking and subsequently ignore them, pre-warn them that you're not being anti-social. Each cockpit and airframe will raise its own potential distractions, but as always, forewarned is forearmed.

Eliminate and Prioritise.

Despite a high level of awareness and preparedness, distractions will always occur as one cannot have control over everything. Accordingly, it's important to deal with distractions appropriately when they arise.

The first step is a simple one – elimination. If the potential distraction is a non-aviation related function, eliminate it. Turn the cell phone off. Even if you choose to supposedly ignore it on the ground, its ringing is an interruption and challenge to your primary task of flying the aeroplane. Some airlines permit phone use on the ground to resolve maintenance issues in multi-crew operations, but there are strict procedures involved regarding stopping the aircraft, parking the brakes and having the other pilot taking control of the aircraft and radios. General aviation aircraft don't really offer that security as a phone call can only compromise the pilot's ability to monitor the many and varied aspects of the aircraft and the surrounding environment. Whether it is a phone, a disorderly passenger, or any other potential distraction to you as pilot-in-command, eliminate it beforehand.

Interruptions are possibly the most frequent distraction. They can come from passengers, air traffic control and even flight instructors. Regaining the flow, can sometimes be difficult and we have all had those, "Now where was I?" moments. If this happens, go back a couple of steps in the process. That may mean doing an engine run a second time or restarting a checklist from the top. Find a known point in the process that you can recall with clarity and start again. If it's a piece of communication, ask them to "say again" or even better "standby" while you gather your thoughts or a pen and paper. You are the pilot in command, so you determine the pace and the direction of the flight and its management at all times.

When unavoidable distractions occur, and they will, it is important to prioritise. To harp on an old favourite, AVIATE-NAVIGATE-COMMUNICATE. Always fly the aeroplane, first and foremost.

When the distraction first occurs, fly the aeroplane and consider, "Is this distraction critical to my phase of flight?" If not, ignore it Two common occurrences over the years have been doors coming open after take-off and seat-belts outside the door banging on the fuselage. Both events can sound dreadful, but are they critical to that phase of flight? They may call for a return to land, but if they aren't impacting upon aircraft controllability, AVIATE-NAVIGATE-COMMUNICATE. Reaching across to try and slam a door or instructing a passenger to do so can only add to the distraction. Fly the aircraft and sort it out after landing.

Always consider, "Is this distraction critical to my phase of flight?" and assess the aircraft's situation; height, speed, attitude, altitude, fuel status, etc. If an unsafe landing gear horn sounds on the approach to land, it is most definitely a critical phase of flight and at an altitude too low to troubleshoot. Go-around, climb to a safe place and assess the fuel status of the aircraft and decide upon a course of action. In this case, the warning horn may prove to be far more than a simple distraction.

In an emergency situation, the number of distractions may increase significantly. More than ever the pilot will need to AVIATE-NAVIGATE-COMMUNICATE and not only resolve the emergency but differentiate between what is a genuine issue and what is merely a distraction. That ability to prioritise is a function of having a sound process, a clear head and a varying amount of experience.

The scenarios are limitless, from sick passengers to talkative passengers and from false warnings to full-blown emergencies. The severity of the event doesn't necessarily determine the degree of the distraction; remember the ill-fated airliner's light bulb? Regardless of its measure, a distraction draws the pilot's focus away from the primary task of flying the aircraft and that can end very badly.

A Fact of Life.

Distractions have always been with us in the cockpit. Their form may be changing in this world of multi-tasking, but they still present the same threat to safety. As pilots, we need to be the filter that traps the distractions and puts them in their place. We can begin with an awareness, while some we can eliminate and some we may need to prioritise. The more that we can manage distractions before they escalate, the safer our flying will be.

We need to recognise them for what they are – distractions. They may be the forebear of a greater emergency, but in the first instance we must always continue to fly the aircraft. Only when it is in a safe place and with adequate fuel in the tanks, can we divert our attention to resolve, manage or dismiss the distraction. Always be the pilot-in-command and never let a simple distraction develop into a disaster.

Points to Remember.

* Technology has brought both assets and potential distractions into the cockpit.

* Become familiar with tablets, Apps and other aids on the ground before flight. Consider a safety pilot on the first flights with a new device.

* Be aware of potential distractions. Eliminate them where possible and prioritise them when necessary.

* As always, Aviate – Navigate – Communicate.

CHAPTER TWENTY

TRANSITIONING TO A NEW AIRCRAFT TYPE.

One of the enjoyable aspects of flying is when we have the chance to fly a new aircraft type. It may be a step up in performance, the ability to travel further, the need for more seats or just a change in flight schools that call for a pilot to become familiar with a different machine. For whichever reason, it's an exciting time, but as always in aviation, it'll call for a little work too.

Choosing the New Machine.

It may seem an odd question at the start of a chapter on changing aircraft, but is the change needed? I remember training many years ago and going through the phase of building command hours to proceed to the next stage of my training. A friend of mine chose to change types at this stage to a four-seater that had a little more speed, while I stayed with the little two-seater, cruising at 100 miles per hour.

He had the expense of training on the new aircraft, which was not command time, and then he had a higher hourly rate as he accrued his solo time. In the end he literally spent thousands of dollars more than me and it was something he told me he regretted.

For the task was to accumulate hours and the size and the speed of the aircraft at this stage was irrelevant. Furthermore, virtually all of the flying was done solo, or with one passenger at most. The back seat remained vacant, but still the hourly rate was higher. The point of this is not to deter, but to encourage an honest assessment of one's needs before handing over hard-earned cash.

Having given the change due consideration, it is now a matter of finding the correct aircraft for the job. More speed requires the aircraft to have a constant speed propeller and possibly, retractable undercarriage. If there is a view to carrying more people, then more seats are obviously needed. If moving into the world of acrobatic flight, then the aircraft must be capable of those manoeuvres and its highly likely that a tailwheel endorsement is worthwhile as many basic and most advanced acrobatic aircraft have the small wheel down at the tail.

At the advanced end of the scale there are multi-engine, turbo-prop and pressurised aircraft to name but a few. However, the issue remains the same - define the need and then find an aircraft configuration that is suitable. And then find which types in this category are available.

Just like when choosing a flight school, do your homework. Read pilot reports on the internet and visit the flight schools to see the aircraft. They may well have information on the aircraft they can give you, as well as the cost of hiring it. It will give you an opportunity to survey the school's facilities and to ask what training they require prior to being able to hire the aircraft.

Importantly, ensure that you sit in the aircraft. Individual physiques are better suited to certain aircraft. Are all the controls and switches, particularly the fuel selector, in easy reach? Is the seat adjustable, or would cushions be needed, or is the cockpit too small with no headroom. If the intention is to predominantly fly the aircraft at night, it may be wise to arrange to see the cockpit and instrument panel lighting once the sun goes down. These are all features that can only be determined by physically sitting in the aircraft. You are the customer and its your money, so do the research before investing.

Getting Familiar.

When an aircraft type has been chosen, preparation is once again the key. It will result in a more competent and enjoyable training experience and very likely save money in the process.

Certain types will have a very defined syllabus and some may even be supported by a simulator. However, in the majority of cases there will be a ground-based theory and airborne practical component. Some schools may ask for less, others more. It may be amazingly simple in some cases, still, to fly any aircraft confidently you need to know it. So even if the school doesn't insist on a 'type course', allow your personal airmanship to demand it.

Familiarising oneself with a new aircraft can start with the associated documentation, well in advance of even flying the aircraft. The aircraft's Flight Manual contains a wealth of information, specific to that aircraft and Pilot Operating Handbooks, or similar, can be acquired for most makes and models.

Understanding the systems is of critical importance, particularly the fuel system. Weight and balance charts offer a better understanding of loading the aircraft while performance charts relate to a vast range of aircraft operating envelopes, notably take-off and landing performance. And of course, there are the emergency procedures.

From the outset, it is worth working some examples to find limiting scenarios that may serve as a warning when the aircraft is approaching its operating limit in some aspect. This does not replace calculating data for the individual flight, but offers a general overview of the aircraft's performance and a gross error check against your more detailed computations.

Some sample scenarios worth noting may include,

- If the fuel tanks are full, how many passengers can be uplifted and is there room for baggage?.
- Conversely, with the aircraft full of passengers, how much fuel can be carried and what range does that offer in still wind conditions?
- On a hot day, how much runway is required to take-off and land at maximum weight and is there a limiting Outside Air Temperature for the aircraft?

Questions like these may also highlight whether this really is the correct aircraft after all as the chosen type may be limited in an aspect of its operation. Also, for all of these general overview calculations, it is worth making the environmental conditions less than favourable to get a feel for the aircraft's performance on hotter days or when a few knots of tailwind sneak up.

The next 'free' step is to sit in the aircraft while it is on the ground and not costing a penny. The first cautionary note is to be aware of the location of the magneto switch, the master switch, landing gear lever and any other switch or lever that can lead to an inadvertent activation and a potentially horrific outcome.

With the checklists in hand, work through everything from the pre-flight inspection to after shutdown and have the manual nearby to answer those deeper questions that may arise. Being comfortable with the location of various switches and dials from the outset is not only comforting, but can assist in keeping distractions to a minimum. Again, the fuel system is critically important from the quantity gauges to the selectors to the boost pump, drain positions and even the type of fuel caps.

This is also an opportunity to examine those less utilised systems such as emergency gear extension, and selection of alternate air or suction sources. Small, lock-wired items that are often tucked away out of sight. More significant are the emergency procedures for the aircraft which may also include such items as emergency door releases or ballistic chutes. Additionally, the location of emergency gear such as first aid kits, portable beacons, life jackets and first aid kits.

Yet for all the major items and emergency procedures, sometimes it can be the little things that can prove awkward when changing types and particularly embarrassing in front of passengers. Door operation, cowling latches, park brake location, instrument dimmer switches, headset jacks, avionics master switch and seat folding or adjustment are just a few of the subtle traps that can vary from aircraft to aircraft.

Whether or not it is required to complete a ground school and a written examination on a particular aircraft type, airmanship dictates that a level of real proficiency should be reached before the wheels ever leave the ground. It'll cost a little time, but it is cheaper, less rushed and more effective than trying to 'learn on the run' in flight.

Taking Flight.

The instructor and the relevant syllabus will determine the minimum requirements to fly a particular aircraft. However, traditionally, a flight check will be composed of an upper air work component of general handling, followed by some time in the circuit. Rather than seeing this flight as a hurdle, like a licence test, it is a real opportunity to glean information from the instructor.

From the engine starting procedure onwards, the new aircraft will present changes – some are obvious and some are very subtle. Even as we taxi, the application of brakes may vary and steering may now be castoring rather than a direct linkage to the nosewheel, or even a tailwheel. Beware that as this may draw a good deal of our mental powers, we still need to monitor the taxiway ahead and our wingtip clearance. The new aircraft may have a greater span, reducing the clearance on familiar hangars or fuel bowsers. If in doubt, stop and get external guidance, or shut down and get out.

It is also a tremendous opportunity to fly the aircraft in non-standard configurations, such as a flapless landing, or a practice engine failure and glide approach or forced landing. As well as becoming more intimate with the new aircraft across a broader range of handling conditions, there is the chance to get some quality input from an instructor.

In the circuit, short field technique will offer a real appreciation of the distance required to take-off and land the aircraft, but as always, be wary. If operating off a dry, sealed runway, the performance may vary greatly from a wet, grass airstrip – so back to the performance charts we go. Entering the circuit can also be a challenge if the new aircraft is of a higher performance. A common error is to enter the circuit too fast, then be unable to slow down to a safe speed to extend the flaps. The knock-on effect is a rushed approach to land. When getting to know a new, higher performance aircraft, slow down early and even have a stage of flap selected before entering the circuit. Speed will come with time, but for the moment, the focus should be on getting the process right. And if it isn't? Then go-around and try again. No shame at all, it's a sound command decision.

If the change in type is also a change in flight schools or even airfields, this flight can be a chance to learn the local procedures and ask questions of the flight instructor before it ever becomes an issue for air traffic control.

As with any flight, the instructor will have feedback and the student questions. However, the time, effort and preparation will all be worthwhile when the new type of aircraft is inked in the log book.

When the process is complete, a pilot is now permitted to fly a new aircraft that may open up a new range of options from the number of passengers that can be carried to the number of miles that can be covered. As always, take care. An old familiar type can sometimes surface and the 'muscle memory' take control, particularly when a pilot is under pressure. A landing gear lever may now be positioned where the flap selector was previously, or the throttles and pitch lever may be swapped around. Don't rush and positively identify every switch and lever before moving it. Regressing to a previous aircraft type is not uncommon, so as always, take the time that is needed.

Cleared for Take-Off.

Transitioning to a new aircraft is a normal progression in any pilot's journey. It is an exciting time that can avail new opportunities. Along the way, these transitions may happen a number of times. Following a process in an unrushed manner is the best way to bed down the new information and safely operate the aircraft. A 'quick check' may be tempting, but it can prove far more costly in the long run.

When the theory is understood and the handling skills are to a safe standard, we can then take to the skies in a new machine with the understanding and competence that gives us the confidence needed and the security that our passengers deserve.

Points to Remember.

* Do you really need to change aircraft types?

* Understand your aircraft's systems – including the 'little things'.

* A quality endorsement on the type is money well spent.

*Beware of 'muscle memory' and regression to a more familiar aeroplane.

CHAPTER TWENTY ONE

WELL CHOSEN WORDS.

The value of pre-flight preparation can never be overstated. The attention to detail before entering the cockpit often dictates the standard of the flight that follows. Within this vast array of activities ranging from flight planning to fuel management exists one critical, but often forgotten task; the verbal briefing.

The Little Things.

Many complex tasks and creations are comprised of numerous smaller items at their core and flying an aeroplane is no different. What appears to be an overwhelming task of co-ordination and orientation to the layman is actually the culmination of numerous components coming together in a careful methodical fashion. Omission of a single item may not be particularly significant, but it can contribute to a snow-balling effect with far more severe consequences. Hence, attention to detail and self-discipline are vital qualities in all aviators.

Executing a flight in an efficient fashion can be assisted greatly by catering for contingencies before they ever eventuate. This might entail carrying enough fuel to divert to an alternate aerodrome, or considering a plan of action in the event of an engine failure. Whatever the contingency may be, the ability to weigh up options and devise a strategy before the event ever occurs is of an immense amount of benefit. Inevitably, when things fail to go as planned, the workload and pressure in the cockpit mount up. If not prepared, the new plan must be hatched on the run with a myriad of other tasks eroding the thought processes. It's a tough situation.

Having a plan etched out in advance can be of enormous value in these situations. The plan doesn't necessarily need to be complex or long-winded, in fact to the contrary, the simpler the better. And while complex procedures can be designed to extract a multi-crew airliner from harm's way following an engine failure after take-off amongst hazardous terrain, a verbal self-brief before take-off can be equally valuable to the private pilot in his 'single'. A few timely words can make all the difference when the chips are down.

Keeping it Simple.

I am sure we have all heard pilots on the radio that love the sound of their own voices. Void of radio etiquette, they ramble on, jamming up the frequency. The fact is that communication is about quality, not quantity and this is a prime consideration when we first consider what needs to be said in a verbal briefing. Whether acting as part of a crew, or flying solo, an overly long briefing often fails to deliver the results. People tune out and the few vital facts can be lost in the background hash of a boring briefing.

The purpose of the briefing is to revisit the key points relating to the upcoming critical phase of flight. Whether before take-off or prior to commencing descent, the briefing serves to rekindle those key numbers and details that we may have to recall in the heat of the moment. It also allows an opportunity to check that the 'house is in order' with navigation aids tuned, the QNH set and so on. For ease of execution, the briefing should ideally be logical in its format; discuss the items in the order that you anticipate they will occur. This permits an easy resumption of the brief in the case of interruption too, although it's always worthwhile to 'back up' a few stages to guard against omissions.

As discussed, over-briefing can be as equally useless as not briefing at all. In fact, it can create time pressure and lead people to talking when they should be flying. Always remember, AVIATE-NAVIGATE-COMMUNICATE. As such, not every phase of flight needs to be spoken about. Generally, the two most critical phases of flight are the departure and the approach and landing. In both instances, there are actions to be considered should the planned manoeuvre suffer a change, such as an engine failure or a possible runway incursion necessitating a go-around.

The key to an effective briefing is to keep it as relevant and as simple as possible. There is no need to re-iterate standard procedures or use fancy grammar. Keep to the facts that you want in your mind at minimum notice and shelve anything that is non-essential.

Say What?

The content of a briefing can be varied depending on so many factors. It may be a multi-crew flight deck or a solo exercise, the flight maybe a VFR single, or an IFR twin. As such, no one text can be definitive and the pilot, aircraft and standard operating procedures will be the ultimate determinants. To that end, while the content needs to be tailored to the operation, the principles of simplicity and relevance remain the same.

Threat management is a bit of a 'catch-cry' these days, but it highlights the numerous potential traps that pilots face and are not limited to the operation of the aircraft. Threats may be Notices to Airmen (NOTAMs), aircraft serviceability, specific aerodrome procedures, significant terrain or even birds migrating at dusk. The list is endless, but for briefing, the list should be limited to the particular threats for this phase of flight. Considering the potential threats is always a good place to start a briefing. From here, evolve the briefing as events will unfold.

Pre-departure, it is worth briefing before engine start if possible. The background noise of the engine and the ticking by of time and fuel has not yet been introduced into the cockpit. Following the consideration of threats, confirm the ATIS and check that the QNH is set correctly. This will also provide an opportunity to assess the wind and whether its impact on take-off technique and a return to land if needed. The taxi route may be complex or infringed by obstacles or active runways and this may need to be considered.

Next the take-off can be discussed, particularly if a short field technique or different flap setting is to be used. Does the terrain play a role in your departure? More complex aircraft may have specific take-off data and 'V Speeds' to review at this point. For the airborne component, consider the departure track, navigation aids and the first assigned altitude. Also, a final check of flight planned fuel against what you *actually* have on board is well worthwhile.

Last, but by no means least, comes the consideration of emergency contingencies. This may include an engine failure on the runway, or after take-off. What landing options lie ahead should the need arise and at what point and height does a return to land at the airfield become a possibility? And, what are the vital actions and critical airspeed to maintain in this situation? Discussing the

THE PRACTICAL PILOT

emergency situation last leaves those key points freshest in your mind should the added pressure of a problem arise. Obviously, the emergency plan will vary depending on such factors as the number of remaining engines in the case of a failure and the weather in the area. Hence, look at your plan realistically.

At the other end of the flight, the descent and approach phase is worth briefing and again it is best to follow a relevant order. Ideally, such a brief should be completed well in advance of commencing the descent. Start with the potential threats for the descent and in the terminal area. Terrain is always worth considering as a threat when you're descending towards it. Review the ATIS, QNH and prevailing weather conditions as this will also provide some insight into the conditions you are likely to be confronted with. Review the descent profile in terms of minimum safe altitudes and circuit joining procedures, before considering the approach to land. Revisit the flap setting to be used, the approach speed, the runway length available and where you anticipate turning off to taxi to the parking area. Importantly, examine the go-around situation. How will it be flown, what fuel will be remaining and what options are available in the event of a missed approach? Flying the missed approach should be thought of in terms of the actual aircraft handling as well as the flight path to be flown. With the period from top of descent to the potential missed approach covered, pilot and aircraft are prepared to start heading down and reunite with the runway ahead.

Multi-engine aircraft and Instrument Flight Rules (IFR) offer more variables. On take-off, you are not likely to make a visual return to land if the cloud base is 200 feet above ground level, so setting up the navaids and having the relevant approach plate at the ready may be prudent in this instance. However, there is no need to brief the approach at this time. Conversely, when considering an instrument approach prior to descent, it is very relevant to thoroughly brief the approach and airfield lighting as well as confirming the readiness of the navigation aids. The weather at the minima also obviously plays a critical role in IFR and should be assessed to give some indication of what will be seen should 'visual reference' be attained right at the minima. For instance, in a strong crosswind and lowered visibility, looking straight ahead might lead to not sighting the runway which is now offset.

Regardless, of the relative simplicity or complexity of the operation, the briefing should remain practical, ordered and relevant to the phase of flight. Many commercial flight providers will define the content of the briefing in their 'Standard Operating Procedures', but for the individual, the choice remains in their hands.

Speak Up.

As a point of technique, briefings should be spoken out aloud. This is obvious in the multi-crew scenario as the information is there to be shared. Equally importantly, the briefing offers the opportunity for other crew members to raise questions and point out any omissions. Through an open briefing technique, all of the flight crew are able to be 'on the same' page and not guessing the next move of the pilot flying.

Even in single pilot operations, there are also definite benefits in briefing out aloud. It may seem strange at first, but the spoken word will allow the content to also be absorbed aurally and not merely through the 'mind's ear'. This provides another layer of consolidation to cement the details in the mind. That is not to say that the briefing needs to be yelled out, but a quiet review to oneself will serve the briefing better.

When flying with passengers, obviously keep the audio level down as words like 'engine failure' can tend to alarm them. However, if simply taking a friend for a flight in the front seat, explain to them what you're doing. In much the same way as you explain the emergency exits to them, reviewing your plan is simply a case of preparing for every situation. Passengers will often be reassured by such thoroughness, as this is in line with cabin briefings on an airliner.

Supporting briefings, pilots may also choose to have a simple checklist to assure that they have covered the content. Additionally, there is a real benefit to be derived from 'touch-drills' for such manoeuvres as an engine failure after take-off. Point at the best glide speed, touch those points associated with the emergency and the flap lever in unison with your words. It is a quick but very effective means of reviewing a very critical manoeuvre.

Ultimately, the technique adopted will be the one with which the pilot is most comfortable and most likely to recall from day to day. Keeping the format constant will assist in guarding against omissions, maintaining a flow and keeping it concise.

Well Chosen Words.

Briefings are a mandatory component of standard operating procedures in airline operations. However, they need not remain the domain of multi-crew flight decks, nor are the benefits limited to heavy jets. Every pilot in every cockpit stands to gain from an enhanced level of mental preparedness. Keeping the content of briefings concise, ordered and relevant will allow critical points to be refreshed in a pilot's memory without the pressure of a critical flight phase bearing down upon them.

Briefings are a relatively simple task, which when practised will become a small but vital tool in the pilot's kit bag. They are not a major burden upon time or resources, but in the heat of the moment a successful outcome may well result from a few well chosen words.

Points to Remember.

* Executing a flight in an efficient fashion can be assisted greatly by catering for contingencies before they ever eventuate.

* Even in single pilot operations, there are also definite benefits in briefing out aloud.

* When flying with passengers, obviously keep the audio level down as words like 'engine failure' can tend to alarm them.

* Every pilot in every cockpit stands to gain from an enhanced level of mental preparedness.

CHAPTER TWENTY TWO

PASSING FLIGHT TESTS AND CHECK RIDES

Check flights are part of the aviation landscape. There are few pilots that enjoy them and there is a great majority that anticipate them with a distinct loathing. Either way, they are another piece of the aviation jigsaw that is necessary to make the picture complete. I have been fortunate to sit in both seats on different occasions; as the examiner and as the candidate. Consequently, over the years I have witnessed both stunning successes in the air and flights that literally never left the ground. As with any aviation skill, at times performance can be a matter of technique. So let's now consider some of those 'techniques', both good and not-so-good.

A Necessary Evil.

Piloting calls for a balance of theoretical knowledge and real world application. Too much of one at the expense of the other is an undesirable situation and we have probably all met examples of this in our travels. Unfortunately, even if we possess the correct blend of mind and muscle, these skills can be eroded by memory and lack of practise. Similarly, each time we seek to upgrade to a higher level of licence or rating, a new set of benchmarks come into play. Even the rules and regulations can change and require vigilance. As a consequence, check flights are the means of verifying that a pilot is competent to hold a particular level of licence. Whether that verification takes place in a two-seat Cessna or a Boeing simulator sitting atop its spider-like hydraulic legs, much of what the examiner seeks to witness and the apprehension the candidate feels is the same in either case. It's all a part of the human condition.

Nerves, Nerves, Nerves.

Before we look at flying the check ride it is best to address the elephant in the room – nervous tension. First and foremost, this is an entirely natural emotion and reflects how important our flying is to us. That being said, a little nervous tension can be beneficial in motivating us and sharpening our senses, but too much can hamper our performance. It's all a matter of degree. For some, the anxiety can slowly begin to build weeks before the test, while for others an acute sense of near panic can strike on the day of the flight. Neither of these are ideal.

A check ride is not an insurmountable task and it is important to give the flight some perspective. Firstly, your instructor must believe that you are of the required standard to put you forward for the test. Secondly, in your own heart, you will know if you have done enough preparation. Also, you are not alone in this, many others have successfully completed the path that you are set to undertake.

Flight examiners know that you are nervous and one of their

objectives before the flight should be to put you at ease. Furthermore, none of us 'fly the perfect flight' but a safe and sound performance is the goal. Later in this chapter, we will discuss some strategies to reduce the stress levels and optimise your performance. For the moment, just remember, you are not alone in feeling nervous. It is a natural response to the situation and just another aspect of flight management that you need to address in a logical, prepared manner.

Be Prepared.

The first step in the process is to be prepared well before the big day arrives. A little time dedicated to study each day can make a huge difference. The aircraft's limitations and critical speeds as well as any memory checklists should be well entrenched. Additionally, the rules and regulations and the privileges of the licence and rating should all be known in advance. These are memory items that can only be learned through repetition, however, learning them can provide a solid dose of self-confidence on the day of the check ride. Particularly, when you can fire back the answers to the examiner without hesitation.

One technique that I use to this day is to record the limitations, speeds and memory drills of my aircraft and listen to them in my car. At every opportunity I listen to this 20-minute recording and definitely each time that I drive to the airport. These are 'must know' items that every examiner will expect to be recalled without difficulty. Consequently, I start this routine as soon as I start flying a new aircraft type to allow the facts and numbers to bake in slowly and well before the test date arrives.

Another consideration is the flight test pro-forma that the examiner uses for the test. This will give an appreciation of what items may be quizzed pre-flight, what exercises are required to be demonstrated in the air and what the flying tolerances may be. (i.e. altitude +/- 100 feet, airspeed +/- 10 knots, or something similar) And while you may hear that certain examiners have pet questions or subjects, be wary of this. A last minute change of examiner or misinformation can leave you rather 'exposed'.

One of the best preparation techniques is always aiming to fly to a standard. Regardless of the flight being undertaken, conduct the same thorough pre-flight routine, apply the highest standard in the execution of the flight and consider a personal debrief afterwards of how the flight may have been better flown. Never hurry or accept short-cuts. Always flying to a standard means that there isn't a step up to test standard, nor should there be. The check ride will be far easier if you fly just as you do each time that you take to the sky.

Pausing after each flight to self-debrief is very beneficial. While the details are still fresh in the mind you are able to recall that radio call or departure procedure that you didn't quite get right. As I said, there is no such thing as a perfect flight, so don't be too hard on yourself in the debrief. Note some points down and remind yourself of them before you next fly. It's a friendly personal reminder and it will make a huge difference to your flying over time.

As the day grows closer, there are some administrative tasks to attend to. Firstly, ensure that you have met all of the legal requirements to undertake the check ride and have had your log book, training file and licence endorsed as needed prior to the day. As an examiner I have encountered a number of instances where flight instructors have not ensured that this was done, so be proactive. It is disappointing for everyone involved when a check ride is cancelled for this reason.

The Big Day.

Preparation. Punctuality. Presentation.

Prior to the big day, your preparation will have consolidated all of the core facts and figures. In the lead up to the flight, begin casting one eye to the weather and relevant Notices to Airmen. Both may change on the day of the flight, but a general overview in advance offers a good backdrop.

The night before, have all of your gear organised and cast an eye over the weather and any briefing material. This may change overnight, but it offers an unpressured read through to highlight any obvious, looming issues. Ensure a good night's sleep is on the agenda and that a good breakfast and adequate sustenance is provided for the next day. I have been guilty previously of getting caught up in the occasion and not eating properly and ultimately this leads to fatigue. Stay hydrated and fed to give your body and brain every chance to perform at their best.

If your flying school calls for you to wear a uniform, then have it cleaned and pressed and shoes shining. If casual clothing is the order of the day, then clean, pressed and comfortable is equally satisfactory.

Arrive at the airfield early and organise as many aspects of the flight as possible. Refuelling and pre-flighting the aircraft, reviewing the weather, flight planning and cleaning the windscreen are all tasks that can be completed prior to the examiner's arrival. By the time you sit down to begin the process you should be ready to go and not rushing. Presenting the examiner with a neatly completed log book, licence and training file that is all in order is a great start.

From experience, I can attest to the fact that a punctual, well presented candidate that is ready to fly is ahead of the game even before the flight test begins. For this may be the first time an examiner meets the candidate and first impressions count. These simple steps can reflect the candidate's degree of self-discipline and organisation. Both are important traits in the cockpit too.

There are frequently a series of questions prior to the flight and that's where a sound study routine can pay dividends. If competent answers are forthcoming, the process can be relatively painless, but if there are obvious gaps in the candidate's knowledge, the examiner is liable to probe ever more deeply. That being said, if you don't know an answer, consider the question for a moment before admitting that you don't know. Never try to conjure an answer unless it can be founded on some strong supporting evidence, even then, admit that you are unsure in this instance.

Both on the ground and in flight, be quietly confident and remember that if you've done the hard work, you should pass. This is not to be confused with over-confidence or arrogance as these qualities tend raise the ire of examiners as they are often little more than false bravado. Equally, you should be appropriately assertive to display that you have what it takes to be the pilot in command of an aircraft. This will become even more important as you progress up through the various levels of licence.

In the air, fly as you have always flown and don't try to second guess what the examiner wants. Prior to a flight test I would always brief certain aspects of the flight from the examiner's perspective. For instance, if I was writing something down, don't panic….it could be something good. If I am quiet, I am not angry, I am simply avoiding interrupting you. Each examiner has a different style, so don't try to change to suit it. You have your style, so stick with it as it has served you well this far.

Throughout the flight, you may be asked questions. If it is at an inappropriate time, then advise the examiner to politely standby and you will address the question after the turning point, radio call, or whatever event is approaching. Some examiners intentionally do this to distract the candidate. Personally, I generally found it to be counterproductive, but be aware that it is a trick of the trade.

If at any stage you make a mistake, then acknowledge it, fix it and carry on. You can't let an error eat at you and the examiner will watch closely for just that. Generally, one mistake in isolation does not constitute a fail assessment, but if mismanaged can lead to an unfortunate cascading series of other issues. I was actually better able to gauge the standard of a pilot by the way that mistakes were managed. We all make mistakes, it is how we recover and carry on that defines us as pilots. After all, we can't drive looking in a rear-view mirror.

Aside from aircraft handling, the examiner will be watching for the ability to make decisions. If the cloud base is getting lower, or the headwinds are eating into your fuel stocks, then make an early and conservative decision. Never sit there simply hoping that things will improve. Once again, it is a reason to always have an awareness of nearby airfields, even if they weren't planned ports of call. On one flight test the candidate opted to land, refuel and wait out some passing weather. The weather wasn't that bad, but there was a positive decision, successfully actioned on the side of safety. It was one of the most impressive flight tests that I was ever privileged to conduct.

As the flight test draws to a close, be aware that fatigue may be sneaking in. Try to freshen up and focus for the home straight to finish on a high note, keeping any silly little errors at bay. The hard work has already been done, so this is the chance to really bring all of your hard work to a successful conclusion.

After the Flight.

It sounds simple, but when you bring the aircraft to a halt at the end of the flight, ensure that you complete your checklists and secure the aircraft. I have commonly had candidates park the aeroplane with the flaps still extended, the strobes flashing or worst of all leaving the magnetos on. It's understandable at the end of a long, tortuous day, but really maintain the focus right until the end.

In the briefing room, ALWAYS be attentive and take notes. The examiner will appreciate the courtesy and some of the most constructive criticism can stem from a good debriefing. Even if the assessment has not been favourable, do not throw the towel in. Keep your chin up and truly show the examiner your strength of conviction. Take on board any suggestions and enact the suggested plan to have the check repeated. Anyone can fail a check – anyone. There is no shame in it and how one recovers and carries on is an indication of true character. There will be anger and frustration and there will be a time and place to express that, but not in the debrief. Even so, never be overly hard on yourself. A fail is painful, but it is a hiccup in the bigger scheme of things. Vent, curse, get angry and then move on, it's behind you and your new licence still lies ahead.

Regardless of the outcome, always be polite and thank the examiner for their time at the end of the debriefing. Aviation is a small industry and your courtesy will be remembered, but so will any indiscretions that may bubble up in the heat of the moment.

As I said from the outset, flight tests and checks are a necessary evil of the aviation landscape. In a professional career, or a lifetime of private flying, there will be occasions when a pilot's proficiency will need to be displayed. It may not be fun, but it is essential and if a pilot has applied themselves and made a genuine effort to reach and maintain the required standing, then the check flight will be successful. And the great majority are successful.

Points to Remember.

* Be prepared, punctual and well presented.

* Always fly to a standard…not just in check flights.

* Being nervous is natural and thorough preparation is the best defence.

* Arrive early and complete as many tasks as possible, before the check flight begins.

* Be decisive and appropriately assertive.

* Be attentive in both the pre-flight and postflight briefings.

One Last Word

Thank you for reading The Practical Pilot.

Please visit www.owenzupp.com for the latest updates.

My other books are listed below;

'Without Precedent' (Hardcover, Paperback, and eBook)

'50 Tales of Flight' From Biplanes to Boeings. (Paperback and eBook)

'50 More Tales of Flight' (Paperback and eBook)

'Solo Flight' One Pilot's Aviation Adventure around Australia (Paperback and eBook)

'Down to Earth' A Fighter Pilot's Experiences of surviving Dunkirk, the Battle of Britain, Dieppe and D-Day. (Grub Street Publishing. 2007)

Aviation is an ongoing process of accumulating experience and knowledge that never ends. As I said at the start of this book, one of the great joys and frustrations is that a pilot will never perfect the art of flight. However, those days when we get close are memorable and those days that we fall short may seem all too frequent.

Thanks again and safe flying.

Owen

Acknowledgements

My heartfelt thanks goes out to every aircraft owner that has let me sit in their aircraft and every pilot that has let me sit beside them. To every instructor, mentor, training and check captain that I have encountered and every fellow enthusiast that I have chatted with over a coffee – thank you. This series of books are your books for as a pilot I am the by-product of all of your lessons and input.

To my wife and children, thank you for your enthusiasm and patience in equal measures.

To my mother and father, thank you for every ounce of advice that you gave me year in, year out. As a son, brother, father and friend I am the by-product of all of your lessons and input.

And without you, the readers, this book would be merely a voice in the wilderness. Your emails, reviews and kind words continue to inspire me to write. You can never underestimate the impact that your support has made to my journey as a writer. Thank you.

As always, please fly safe.

Cheers

Owen

www.ingramcontent.com/pod-product-compliance
Lightning Source LLC
Chambersburg PA
CBHW070559010526
44118CB00012B/1381